MUSIC AND MUSICIANS
IN
EARLY NINETEENTH-CENTURY CORNWALL

'A Musical Club', Truro 1808
Royal Institution of Cornwall

MUSIC AND MUSICIANS IN EARLY NINETEENTH-CENTURY CORNWALL

The world of Joseph Emidy –
slave, violinist and composer

by

Richard McGrady

University of Exeter Press

First published in 1991 by
University of Exeter Press
Reed Hall
Streatham Drive
Exeter EX4 4QR
UK

Typeset by Kestrel Data, Exeter
Printed in the UK by Short Run Press Ltd, Exeter

British Library Cataloguing in Publication Data
McGrady, Richard
  Music and musicians in early nineteenth century Cornwall:
  the world of Joseph Emidy, slave, violinist and composer.
  1. Music. Cornwall (England)
  I. Title
  780.92

ISBN 0-85989-359-6

CONTENTS

Foreword   vii

Prologue   The Native of Portugal   1

PART ONE: 1775–1799

1   The Slave: Portugal and the Guinea Coast   15
2   *The Indefatigable*   23

PART TWO: CORNWALL 1799–1835

3   New Life: Falmouth   39
4   A 'display of Beauty, Rank and Fashion':
               Cornwall's First Music Festivals   48
5   Truro: Assemblies, Balls and Concerts   63
6   'So innocent yet so fascinating an amusement . . .':
               Concerts across the County   77

PART THREE: CHURCH AND CHAPEL

7   'A strain so grand and impressive':
               The Church and its Music   89
8   Bennett Swaffield and the St. Austell Choir   103
9   'None but persons of ability and good moral
               conduct need apply': Organs and organists   109

PART FOUR: THE THEATRE

10   'A moral and instructive school of rational
               entertainment': The Theatre   127
Epilogue   The Lost Composer   143

Appendix A   The Byfield Organ in St. Mary's Parish Church,
              Truro   150
Appendix B   Composers mentioned in concert reports   152
Notes   156
Select Bibliography   162
Index   165

Principal Abbreviations

JRIC   *Journal of the Royal Institution of Cornwall*
WB   *West Briton*
RCG   *Royal Cornwall Gazette*

List of Illustrations

Anon: 'A Musical Club', Truro 1808   Frontispiece
James Silk Buckingham 1786–1865   11
William Owen: Portrait of Sir Edward Pellew, 1st Viscount Exmouth   22
Ebenezer Collis: Destruction of the *Droits de l'Homme*   31
Nicholas Pocock: Falmouth Harbour   38
Truro 1816   62
Original design for the facade of the Assembly Rooms and Theatre,
Truro   78
Engraving by Samuel Cousins from the painting of Henry Howard:
Davies Gilbert, President of the Royal Society   94
St. Austell Parish Church, 1822   104
A view over Truro from the churchyard of Kenwyn Parish Church,
1806   147

Illustration Acknowledgements

Permission to reproduce material in the possession of the following
Institutions is gratefully acknowledeged: the National Maritime
Museum, London; the Royal Institution of Cornwall.

FOREWORD

The social history of music in Cornwall has yet to be written; in this respect the region has much in common with the rest of Britain. This study began as an attempt to gather the available material from the early nineteenth century and to build up a picture of music and social activities at a time when Cornwall, like much of the nation, was undergoing a period of change and when musical tastes, the demand for entertainment and the place of music in the church were in a particularly interesting phase. A surprisingly lively picture appeared; more significantly, as the material grew, there emerged a story so strange and unexpected that to write a social history alone appeared inadequate. In the following pages these two themes, the story of Joseph Emidy—slave, violinist and composer—and the musical activities which framed his life in this country are woven together.

Many people—too numerous to acknowledge individually—have helped me, suggesting from their own expertise new directions to follow in attempting to rediscover these events. A special debt of thanks, shared I am certain by all who undertake research in Cornwall, is owed to the unfailing courtesy, assistance and advice of the Curator and staff of the Royal Institution of Cornwall.

Richard McGrady

PROLOGUE

The Native of Portugal

I

HERE LIE DEPOSITED
The mortal remains of
Mr. Josh. Antonia Emidy
who departed this life
on the 23rd of April
1835
Aged 60 YEARS
And sacred to whose memory
this tribute of affection is erected
by his surviving family.
He was a native of PORTUGAL
which Country he quitted about
forty years since; and pursuing
the Musical profession resided in
Cornwall until the close of
his earthly Career

Devoted to thy soul inspiring strains
Sweet Music! thee he haild his chief delight
And with fond zeal that shunn'd not toil nor pain
His talent soar'd and genius marked his flight.
In harmony he lived in peace with all,
Took his departure from this world of woe
And here his rest, till the last Trumpet call
Shall make Mankind to joys that endless flow.

The tombstone which tells the bare facts of this curious story stands deep
in the shade of a fir tree in the graveyard of Kenwyn Parish Church on the
outskirts of Truro in the county of Cornwall. The tree has protected the

stone against many years of weathering, though the growth of lichen and
ivy makes some of the words difficult to decipher. The legend is strangely
reticent about the dramatic life it so blandly records. There is much to
intrigue and astonish those who attempt to discover more about Joseph
Emidy who apparently led a tranquil life devoted to music in a country
far from the land of his birth. Emidy was a violinist much admired by all
who came in contact with him; more than this, he was a composer of
orchestral and chamber music—all of which has now disappeared—who
pursued his career as a professional musician in Cornwall. This is a
puzzling choice for one whose roots lay elsewhere; there were, as we shall
see, few obvious attractions or signs of artistic activity to encourage a skilled
instrumentalist or composer to settle in the far South West of England. Why
should a 'native of Portugal'—for so the tombstone describes him—opt to
move from a capital city where cultural activities were numerous to scratch
a living in small towns? As the searcher begins to piece together the story
it becomes apparent that Emidy had no choice in the decision, but the
reason for his move is more dramatic than one could imagine. If the stone
memorial is discreetly reticent about this, it is also silent about another
remarkable aspect of Emidy; though part of his early life was spent in
Portugal, he had been born on the West Coast of Africa and first brought
to Europe as part of the trade in slaves.

Already the story begins to take on unusual aspects; the truth is indeed
stranger than fiction. Any novelist who invented the story of Joseph Emidy
would stretch the reader's credulity to its limits.

There is a second theme against which this unusual and poignant story
must be set, the pattern of entertainments and amusements enjoyed by a
provincial society—and a geographically remote society at that—in the
early nineteenth century. Writers about music, literature and the visual arts
are normally principally—and very properly—concerned about the major
figures of their art; the great composers, writers and painters who enriched
the lives of their contemporaries and who continue to enrich ours; other
writers also concern themselves—again very properly—with those societies
such as Renaissance Italy or eighteenth-century Vienna which produced a
flowering of many individual talents simultaneously. Communities where
no such flowering took place often escape attention. These societies are
normally studied by historians who have other interests; the changing social
and religious organisations, developments of industry and trade and the
details of daily life reflected in buildings and documents are more frequently considered than the more ephemeral delights of the arts, pleasure
and entertainment. Perhaps because these activities *are* ephemeral, the task
is a difficult one; fleetingly caught in a newspaper account or personal

memoir, these events are nevertheless worth attempting to trace. Through these records we can see how the great movements in art filtered through society, how local interests changed—perhaps through the influence of a single individual—and how tastes were formed and altered. Artistic activity can be considered as one important factor in the well-being, or otherwise, of a society; its presence or absence can illuminate many different aspects of a community's character. Even more tellingly, a brief aside in a letter or memoir can bring to life the picture of a social fabric long dead.

Thus, in these pages, Joseph Emidy's unusual personal history is related against some aspects of the life and musical times of his adopted home. In some of these activities—concerts, balls and assemblies—he played an important part; in others, such as the church and the theatre, he may have had much less involvement.

II

Though the picture of musical life in Cornwall which emerges is not one of great activity, it would be a mistake to view it in complete isolation from the rest of Great Britain. Unlike some European countries, the British Isles never enjoyed a wide base of professional musical activities; if one thinks of the wide-spread development of music in Renaissance Italy where many city states—Florence, Rome, Venice, Bologna, Mantua to name only a few at random—had flourishing artistic communities in which music played an important part, the concentration of English musical life around the court looks narrow and restricted in its variety and diversity. Music and its performance have always been costly enterprises needing a wealthy patron—a prince of state or church—to finance its undertaking. In the eighteenth century as the old system of individual aristocratic patronage gave way to new patterns with the rise of public concerts financed by the subscriptions from the increasingly affluent middle classes, English music life tended to remain very centralised. Germany and Austria could produce many cities where a combination of wealthy individuals or public subscriptions could support a flourishing musical establishment drawing excellent performers and resident or visiting composers—Vienna, Salzburg, Berlin, Mannheim, Leipzig, Linz, Hanover . . . the list is too long to continue. In the late eighteenth century England had only two centres of excellence—London and Bath—and they both served much the same audience. The wealthy would travel from their provincial homes to enjoy the London season before moving on to the pleasures of Bath. Though some larger cities had established musical societies which could offer sufficient work to attract touring artists, professional musicians of any distinction moved—with their audiences—on the peripatetic rounds between Bath and London creating a pattern almost as regular as the seasons themselves.

Back in their own communities, those with sufficient wealth to follow the social season might seek to organise events to fill the gaps in the calendar; those with less wealth or opportunity to be part of the fashionable elite would certainly wish to enjoy locally the diversions which, in this class and wealth conscious age, their social betters found in Bath and the capital. Perhaps because of its relatively compact size, such a social pattern was possible in England, though there is little doubt that the more remote regions of the kingdom were conscious of a feeling of isolation. It was not simply distance and the difficulties and cost of travel, though these would play a part; the social elite of Cornwall certainly found time and money to enjoy the Season. More subtle factors were at play. Those with strong political aspirations had long found it advantageous to build their homes close to the capital; to be close to court and the major financial and political institutions meant the reality of being close to the seats of power. Influence, wealth and the opportunity to enjoy the indulgence and ostentation of pleasure concentrated the centralisation further, with a continual draining of the sort of patronage which could support and promote art away from the more distant regions. Cornwall has no houses or establishments on the grand scale; though the local gentry built several charming and attractive country seats over the centuries, none was sufficiently large to support a musical establishment. Though there is evidence that music was enjoyed and practised within many of these houses, it was generally within a domestic, private setting involving the family and close friends.

One source of excellence did maintain more local roots; though their fortunes were subject to continual change, the cathedral cities usually had a stronger musical tradition than other towns of a similar size. The presence of trained organists, choir masters and singers in a community could often provide a focus for other musical activities, though this was not invariably true. In this respect Cornwall was also deprived as the cathedral city of the diocese, Exeter, was the best part of a hundred miles distance from the county's largest centres of population. Parish churches were rarely a substitute in providing a wider artistic stimulation.

In all these respects Cornwall was not unique in the kingdom; like many similar regions remote from major centres it had to create its own pattern of entertainments dependent upon the activities of close-knit communities. Some of the social diversions reflected the larger centres of fashion but took on a distinctly localised flavour.

III

Many statistics can be found to illustrate the difficulties and cost of travel which contributed to the isolation of Cornwall. The *Universal British Directory* of 1791 records that four coaches a week left Falmouth for London, departing at six in the morning and arriving in the capital at 2 pm. on the following day, after overnight stops at the London Inn, Exeter. Over the years rival companies undertook the service, but the length of the journey remained daunting. The *Western Subscription Coach*, for example, took forty one hours to complete the journey from Falmouth to London at a cost of £5 4s. for those taking the journey inside; if a traveller was prepared to face the elements and sit with the coachman and guards outside the fare was £2 18s. [WB 17 November 1815]. This was a substantial fare which could be afforded only by the rich. Shorter journeys were also expensive and lengthy. Falmouth to Exeter took sixteen hours and the journey from Truro to Torpoint in 1820 cost sixteen shillings inside, or ten shillings outside. Allowing for the deterioration of the already poor roads in wet weather and the continual danger of robbery implicit in the presence of armed guards on the coach, extended journeys can rarely have been considered an enticing prospect. For those for whom travel was a necessity there was always the prospect of a trip on the Russell carrier; this was a slower, but cheaper, wagon, accompanied by a military guard, which made regular journeys with munitions and goods from Falmouth. The journey to London took four days and was undertaken twice weekly.

Travel by sea was a realistic alternative; sailing ships made frequent journeys round the coast and it was by this means that much of the commercial trade was conducted. Passengers could travel aboard these ships whose main function was to bring to the Cornish merchants the latest merchandise—everything from fashions and the new novels to pianofortes —from the London dealers. The voyage was of course subject to delays and dangers from storms in the Channel and, even in good conditions, took longer than by road. There were other perils; the safety of all shipping was precarious during the period of the wars with France, and new technology did not always bring the desired results. The trials of a steam packet, *Sir Francis Drake*, reported in the *West Briton* in September 1823, suffered mechanical breakdown on a journey from Portsmouth to Plymouth; half of the sixty passengers, 'many of them of first respectability', left the ship at Start Point when it had to return under canvas for major work to repair the engines which had been blocked by wood chippings and a piece of deal.

In spite of the problems attendant upon long journeys there are nevertheless many indications that Cornwall at the turn of the eighteenth and nineteenth centuries was becoming less isolated than it had ever been before. One factor was indeed the attraction of its remoteness and beauty which captured the imagination of travellers in the spirit of the new Romantic age and opened up such areas as the Lake District and the Scottish Highlands to those in search of new experiences. There is some evidence that Cornwall itself began to share in this new taste.

> The mildness of our winters on the Southern shores of Cornwall, and the salutary effect of so soft and genial an atmosphere on the delicate constitutions of valetudinarians, is daily becoming more apparent, and more attractive. There are at this moment a great many visitors of rank and fashion, who stealing from the hackneyed watering places of the eastern and northern parts of the Kingdom, and the foul air of the Metropolis, have taken up their residence for the winter in this county, which a respectable physician long ago denominated the Montpelier of England. Here they enjoy a mild climate, romantic and ever varying view, cheap markets, and the first medical advice. These comforts are nowhere more apparent than in the pleasant village of Flushing, near Falmouth, which has lately become a favorite residence, and now boasts of many visitors of the first respectability.[1]

Though the new tourism did not supplant the traditional industries—mining, the sea and agriculture—upon which the local economy was built, it did begin to have an important influence upon social life; romantic scenery and a mild climate were all very well, but a fashionable traveller would also look for fashionable entertainment.

Even more significant in contributing to changes of social life was the increased presence of large naval and military communities during the period of the wars with France from the early 1790s. The position of Falmouth as the most westerly port in the kingdom had long been an important factor in its development. The description of the town in *The Universal British Directory* gives a vivid picture of its commercial importance in 1791.

> It is so commodious a harbour, that ships of greatest burden come up to its quay; and there is such a shelter in the many creeks belonging to it, that the whole royal navy may ride safe here in any wind. . . . It is well built, and its trade is considerably increased since the establishment of the packet-boats here for Spain and Portugal, and the West Indies, which not only bring vast

quantities of gold in specie and in bars on account of the merchants in London, but the Falmouth merchants trade with the Portuguese in ships of their own; and they have a great share also in the gainful pilchard trade. It is true, part of this trade was founded in a clandestine commerce carried on by the said packets at Lisbon, where, being the king's ships, and claiming the privilege of not being searched or visited by the custom-house officers, they found means to carry off great quantities of British manufactures, which they sold to the Portuguese, and they conveyed them on shore, as it is supposed, without paying custom. But the government there getting intelligence of it, and complaint being made in England also, where it was found to be prejudicial to the fair merchant, that trade has been effectually stopped.

The choice of Falmouth by the General Post Office as a base for its Spanish mail boats in 1688 immediately raised the status of the port; the service was extended by Packet ships sailing to the West Indies and, by the middle of the eighteenth century, to North America. In the early years of the nineteenth century between thirty and forty sloops were based at Falmouth with their attendant crews—officers, surgeons and sailors—living in the town and the nearby small villages along the creeks of the Fal. Though the primary duties of the ships were to carry the mail, the captains were allowed, for their own profit, to carry fare-paying passengers, and the town became a centre for travellers wishing to join one of the weekly sailings for Lisbon or the monthly trips to the West Indies, North America or other destinations. Supporting services—ship building and refitting yards, sail and rope makers and inn-keepers catering for the needs of passengers—transformed the character of the town into a bustling port. Contact with the wider world also introduced a cosmopolitan atmosphere to the town, typical of any busy sea-port.

Little however was offered in the way of diversions for the more sophisticated traveller who passed through the town. William Beckford spent a week in Falmouth in March 1787 as he awaited passage to Lisbon.

> The glass is sinking; the west wind gently breathing upon the water, the smoke softly descending into the room, and sailors yawning dismally at the door of every ale-house.
> Navigation seems at a full stop. The captains lounging about with their hands in their pockets, and passengers idling at billiards.[2]

Local society appeared unwelcoming to the visitor; the Quaker assembly looked with 'sober and silent dismay' at a visitor 'jingling his fine Geneva watch chains', so Beckford took opportunity to explore the surrounding region; Gwennap parish appeared 'a bleak desert, rendered still more

doleful by the unhealthy appearance of its inhabitants', though the miners
appeared to have unexpected wealth;

> Like sailors in the first effusion of prize-money, they have no notion of turning
> their good luck to advantage; but squander the fruits of their toil in the silliest
> species of extravagance. Their wives are dressed in tawdry silks, and flaunt
> away in ale-houses between rows of obedient fiddlers. The money spent,
> down they sink again into damps and darkness.[3]

In the town cock-fighting and billiards were the only diversions available;

> . . . what can a being of my turn do at Falmouth? I have little taste for the
> explanation of fire-engines, Mr. Scott; the pursuit of hares under the auspices
> of young Trefusis; or the gliding of billiard balls in the society of Barbadoes
> Creoles and packet-boat captains.[4]

The strategic significance of Falmouth took on an even more important
aspect as the situation with France deteriorated into war in the 1790s and
the town became the centre of a major naval presence, second only to
Portsmouth. A substantial community of naval officers and their families
was based in the town with enormous impact upon the nature of the social
life. Other Cornish towns saw a change in their social fabric following the
building of barracks as at Truro, or by providing temporary accommodation for military companies in their movements along the roads. The
atmosphere of war certainly affected the tone of life for the county was in
a front-line position and the fear of invasion could not be escaped. Soldiers,
sailors and French prisoners were a daily sight and provided a constant
reminder of the impending danger. The anticipated invasion affected many
aspects of life. The memoirs of Jonathan Couch of Polperro catch the mood;

> Companies of volunteers were formed in all directions; and those who were
> not actually enrolled, had some specific duty assigned to them in case of
> invasion: such as driving cattle and goods, setting fire to corn, etc.. I remember
> some honest-hearted individuals who lived in continued fear, dreading to go
> to bed lest they should awake at the sound of the trumpet, or in the midst
> of the French troops.[5]

Couch tells of another unexpected result of the situation in France:

> At Pelynt I began the study of Latin, under the care of an emigrant Popish
> priest, one who had escaped from the horrors of the French revolution with
> the skin of his teeth . . .[6]

The movement of troops and prisoners was a frequent sight. John Skinners's departure from Falmouth to Truro in November 1797 was detained for more than an hour by the movement of two hundred and eighty French prisoners under the command of Sir Edward Pellew; the surly behaviour of the French officers and their apparent lack of breeding did not commend them to him and a similar xenophobia is apparent in the account of James Forbes' visit to Cornwall in 1794. In Bodmin—'a poor decayed place'—Forbes encountered French prisoners housed in the new prison which, he felt, was the best building of which the town could boast. Like Skinner, Forbes was not impressed by their appearance or manners.

> Bodmin is at present the receptacle for a number of French officers and other prisoners, on their parole of honor—a few of them may be gentlemen but the generality are a set of ill-looking men, without the least pretension to even the outward appearance of politeness, they were once famous for. They walk about the streets with an air of insolence and contempt, and hold associations to disseminate as much as they can with impunity those pernicious seeds which have spread so deep a root and produced such dreadful fruits in France. At first their plausible system seemed to make an impression on the minds of many of the Bodmin people; it has however since worn off, altho there are still too many of those who ought to know better, tinctured with democratic principles.[7]

For something like twenty years from the beginning of the French wars until the peace settlement in 1814 Cornwall was firmly in the front-line: in addition to the trade links with Portugal, Spain, the West Indies and Brazil the strong naval presence, concentrated upon Falmouth but affecting the whole area, brought the region into the forefront of public affairs in a way which it had never before experienced. Changes in the social order were inevitable.

IV

The circumstances which brought Joseph Emidy to this community are most fully told by James Silk Buckingham. Buckingham, born in Flushing in 1786, achieved distinction in a political career and published his autobiography in 1855. After an account of his childhood and early unsatisfactory experiences in trying to join the legal profession, he returned to Falmouth in his late teens to enjoy two years devoted to pleasure and self-improvement, with the support of his 'fond and indulgent parent'.[8] As part of his plan for self-improvement, he decided that some form of musical accomplishment should be developed; in this wish he had a very practical end in view.

> During this period I began the study of music, finding it a most agreeable recommendation in female society, of which I was always fond; and as I decided to be placed as speedily as possible in the way of turning this acquisition to practical account, I selected the flute as the instrument on which tolerable perfection is soonest attained, and as having the further advantage of portability and convenience. The only teacher procurable at Falmouth was an African negro, named Emidee, who was a general proficient in the art, an exquisite violinist, a good composer, who led at all the concerts of the county, and who taught equally well the piano, violin, violoncello, clarionet and flute. I placed myself under his tuition for an hour's daily lesson under his own eye, and four hours' daily practice beside . . .

The young pupil's musical progress was swift following such a dedicated regime. In two months he was able to play flute solos with the piano, in three months to take the principal flute part in the local orchestra, and in six months

> to play Hoffmeister's Grand Concerto in D, with full orchestral accompaniments, which I did with great *eclat* in one of the monthly concerts of the Harmonic Society of Falmouth, held in the Town Hall . . .

Buckingham refrains from telling us whether he was as successful with the ladies as he was with his flute playing.

It will be noticed that this account reveals a fact which Emidy's tombstone conceals; in the graveyard he is described as 'a native of Portugal' whereas Buckingham identifies him unequivocally as 'an African negro'.

The period of study with Emidy had another important impact upon the author's life. In learning the young musician's life story, which he partially recounts up to 1807 in his *Autobiography*, he developed a sympathy not merely for the African and the treatment which he had received, but for the plight of slaves in general, and, in his later political career, Buckingham remained a fierce opponent of the slave trade and a positive voice for the more just treatment of oppressed people.

James Silk Buckingham 1786–1865
Royal Institution of Cornwall

PART ONE

1775–1799

1

The Slave: Portugal and the Guinea Coast

Buckingham's account adds further details of Emidy's early years to the information on his gravestone.

> He was born in Guinea, on the West Coast of Africa, sold into slavery to some Portuguese traders, taken by them to Brazil when quite a boy, and ultimately came to Lisbon with his owner or master.

Emidy can only have been, at most, in his early teens, and probably was much younger when he was taken from his homeland. To document one child amongst the many thousands snatched from the West Coast of Africa and taken into slavery is impossible. In the second half of the eighteenth century many European nations were involved in the trade and the Portuguese had a long history of involvement. The Portuguese navigators of the fifteenth century had sailed south for trade, not conquest as their Spanish neighbours had; in opening new routes to Asia they traded in gold, spices and slaves. Over the centuries the majority of their slaves, largely bought from native merchants rather than captured by raiding parties, and, much to the amusement of the English slave traders, baptised before shipment,[1] were transported to Brazil to work upon the sugar and tobacco plantations. It was not only their attempt to care for the slaves' souls by baptism which gave the Portuguese the reputation of more humane treatment than the traders of other nations; many were converted to Christianity in Brazil to allow them to take part in the social life of the country which was entirely centred round the church; blacks and whites could mix freely and slaves were given their own plots of land to cultivate and allowed to sell their produce in the markets. Many ultimately won their freedom. Small gestures, in truth, compared with the barbarity of the practice, but greater than those enjoyed by many other slaves. The slave trade with Brazil reached its peak in the last decade of the eighteenth century when 221,000 Africans were transported by the Portuguese; in the decade between 1780 and 1790—the most likely period for Emidy's transportation—the figures were slightly fewer, 178,100, the majority being taken from Angola.[2]

As with all the early events of Emidy's life, the circumstances surrounding the move from Brazil to Lisbon are unlikely ever to be discovered. We know from his gravestone that he was born about 1775 so, as a child or young teenager, it is possible that he was used as a personal attendant rather than for his physical strength on the cotton or tobacco plantations. In the Portuguese Court black slaves were a fashionable adornment; after attending a performance at the *Teatro do Salitre* in November 1787, William Beckford observed:

> It is the high ton at present in this court to be surrounded by African implings, the more hideous, the more prized, and to bedizen them in the most expensive manner.[3]

The behaviour of the 'implings' was as diverting to the audience as the ballet itself.

> Shall I confess that this nonsense amused me pretty nearly as much as it did my companions, whose raptures were only exceeded by those of Madame de Pombeiro's implings. They, sweet, sooty innocents, kept gibbering and pointing at the man with the black compasses in a manner so completely African and ludicrous, that I thought their contortions the best part of the entertainment.[4]

Where fashion leads—especially in so inward-looking a court as that of Maria I—society often follows and it may be that Emidy's master was as much following social patterns as serving practical needs in keeping the boy as his personal attendant.

Emidy's treatment, as described by Buckingham, appears to have been unusually encouraging:

> Here [in Lisbon] he manifested such a love for music, that he was supplied with a violin and a teacher; and in the course of three or four years he became sufficiently proficient to be admitted as one of the second violins in the orchestra of the opera at Lisbon.

These details are intriguing and puzzling; as we shall see, Emidy certainly left Lisbon in 1795 when he was already a member of a Lisbon opera orchestra; for a man in his early twenties, this is already a notable achievement after so short a period—three or four years—of playing his instrument; for a slave whose experience of European cultural traditions can only have been brief, it is a remarkable reflection upon his natural talent. It is moreover a tribute to the liberality of his slave-master to allow the young man to develop his talent, to provide an instrument and instruction—by no means inexpensive commodities—and to permit him to undertake employment as a professional musician.

Lisbon itself was a city of contradictions. It still showed the signs of the disastrous earthquake which, together with the ensuing tidal wave, brought destruction and death upon All Saints' Day, 1755. In the aftermath of the event many residents feared to live in stone buildings and even the Royal family occupied wooden buildings for many years.[5] William Beckford's descriptions of the city—and of his experiences of Falmouth—have already been quoted. He provides many vivid glimpses of Lisbon where he spent much of 1787. Beckford had left England following accusations of scandalous behaviour concerning his relationship with William Courtney of Powderham, published in *The Morning Herald* on 27 November 1784. Though ostracised by the English community, he moved freely in Portuguese society, recording his observations of life, fashion, religion and the arts in a two volume journal, *Italy with Sketches of Spain and Portugal*, which was published in 1834. Beckford was particularly aware of the climate of the capital and the very individual life style which it produced.

> The heat seems not only to have new venomed the stings of the fleas and the musquitoes, but to have drawn out, the whole night long, all the human ephemera of Lisbon. They frisk and dance, and tinkle their guitars from sunset to sunrise. The dogs, too, keep yelping and howling without intermission; and what with the bellowing of litanies by parochial processions, the whizzing of fireworks, . . . and the squabbles of bullying rake-hells, who scour the streets in search of adventures, there is no getting a wink of sleep, even if the heat would allow it.[6]

The packs of wild dogs which roamed the city were one of the after effects of the earthquake. Night could however cast its magic over the city:

> The flights of steps, terraces, chapels, and porticos of several convents and palaces on the brink of the river, shone forth like edifices of white marble, whilst the rough cliffs and miserable sheds rising above them were lost in dark shadows.[7]

As a man of artistic tastes, Beckford was responsive to the music which played a part in most social events. On occasions he was highly critical;

grotesque music—'a sonata on the dulcimer, accompanied on the jews-harp by a couple of dwarfs'—provided the unsatisfactory accompaniment to a dinner at the Anjeja Palace.[8] He was also unmoved by a party of visiting musicians who performed instrumental music in his lodgings:

> a fiddler, a priest, and an Italian musician [who] fell a thumping my poor pianoforte, and playing sonatas whether I would or not. You are aware I am no great friend to sonatas, and that certain chromatic, squeaking tones of a fiddle, when the performer turns up the whites of his eyes, waggles a greasy chin, and affects ecstasies, set my teeth on edge.[9]

Some church music exhibited deficiencies of taste which affected Beckford's susceptibilities:

> A prelate of the first rank, with a considerable detachment of priests from the royal chapel, officiated to the sounds of lively jigs and ranting minuets, better calculated to set a parcel of water-drinkers a dancing in a pump room, than to direct the movements of a pontiff and his assistants.
>   After much indifferent music, vocal and instrumental, performed full gallop in the most rapid allegro Frè Joaô Jacinto, a famous preacher, mounted the pulpit, lifted up hands and eyes, and poured forth a torrent of sounding phrases in honour of St. Anthony. . . . The sermon ended, fiddling began anew with redoubled vigour, and I, disgusted with such unseasonable levity, retired home in dudgeon.[10]

The Queen's chapel, however, could provide musical excellence which compared favourably with any European establishment.

> in point of vocal and instrumental excellence, no other establishment of the kind, the papal not excepted, can boast such an assemblage of admirable musicians . . . She is surrounded by a bevy of delicate warblers, as plump as quails, and as gurgling and melodious as nightingales. The violins and violoncellos at her Majesty's beck are all of the first order, and in oboe and flute players her musical menagerie is unrivalled.[11]

The religious fervour which marked the Queen's court had its impact upon the quality of music composed for the church at a period when, throughout much of Europe, sacred music was in decline at the expense of the new taste for orchestral symphonic music. After hearing a setting of the Matins by Perez and a Requiem by Jommelli at the Church of Martyrs, Beckford wrote:

such august, such affecting music I never heard, and perhaps may never hear again; for the flame of devout enthusiasm burns dim in almost every part of Europe and threatens total extinction in a very few years. As yet it glows in Lisbon, and produced this day the most striking musical effect.[12]

The music and the atmosphere

shook every nerve in my frame, and called up in my recollection so many affecting images, that I could not refrain from tears.[13]

It was not only in the formal setting of a religious service that music of exquisite beauty and magic could occur. A fine young singer, performing songs by Perez with taste and naturalness could move Beckford:

her voice modulates with unaffected carelessness into the most pathetic tones. Though she has adopted the masterly and scientific style of Ferracuti, one of the first singers in the Queen's service, she gives a simplicity of expression to the most difficult passages, that makes them appear the effusions of a young romantic warbling to herself in the secret recesses of a forest.[14]

Spontaneity and simplicity, together with the appropriateness of the setting, appear to have been the qualities to which Beckford responded most strongly; attending a rehearsal of open-air music for the Queen's visit to the Marialva villa in Cintra, he enjoyed

the plaintive tones of voices and wind instruments issuing from the thickets . . . It was one of those serene and genial nights when music acquires a double charm, and opens the heart to tender, though melancholy impressions.[15]

Perhaps it was the exotic novelty of the music, so different from the folk music of England, which provoked such a strong response when Beckford heard a two young women singers, accompanied by their singing-master, 'warbling' Brazilian *modinhas*:

the most bewitching melodies that ever existed since the days of the Sybarites. They consist of languid interrupted measures, as if the breath was gone with excess of rapture, and the soul panting to meet the kindred soul of some beloved object.[16]

In addition to her devotion to the Church, the Queen had a passion for opera. The attendance at the newly built *Teatro do Salitre* with her entourage of 'implings' and her favourite black dwarf, Donna Rosa, has already been noticed in Beckford's account of his visit to the theatre. The *Teatro do Salitre*, opened in 1785, was the most fashionable of the Lisbon theatres in the 1780s and, like most establishments of its period, offered a mixed diet of entertainment: on Beckford's visit in November, 1787, the programme included 'a ranting prose tragedy, two ballets, a pastoral, and a farce'.[17] The theatre however was not the only one in the city which offered opera and ballet as part of its programme. The Royal Palace Theatre, the *Academia da Trinidade* and the *Teatro do Bairro Alto* all included musical entertainment during the 1780s, and in 1793 a new establishment, the *S.Carlos*, opened with an opera by Cimarosa. Any one of these could have qualified for the 'Lisbon Opera' which Buckingham mentions, for each establishment had an orchestra where the young Emidy could have found employment.

As with so much of Lisbon society, the contradictions of taste and fashion caught Beckford's attention. Women were forbidden to appear on the Portuguese stage; in plays, operas and ballets, their parts were undertaken by boys; the effect could be strange.

> [the female parts] are acted by calvish young fellows. Judge what a pleasing effect this metamorphosis must produce, especially in the dances, where one sees a stout shepherdess in virgin white, with a soft blue beard, and a prominent collar-bone, clutching a nosegay in a fist that would have knocked down Goliath.[18]

Even though to most seasoned musical travellers, the concept of the male soprano, the *castrato*, taking the leading *male* role was very familiar in the 1780s, though the practice was on the wane, the unfamiliarity of the male singer undertaking *female* parts was sufficient novelty to call for comment from those familiar with the more liberal traditions in other European centres:

> ... another hob-e-di-hoy, tottering on high-heeled shoes, represented her Egyptian majesty, and warbled two airs with all the nauseous sweetness of a fluted falsetto.[19]

To a young man of Emidy's background, growing up in Lisbon, many of the ambiguities which so struck Beckford can have made little impression. The variety of musical idioms from the ceremonial music of the church, the vividness of the theatre to the haunting character of Brazilian *modinhas* and the nocturnal 'tinkling' of guitars must have offered a rich panoply of experience. Moreover it was a city and society in which his colour was not likely to prove any handicap to the development of his

talents. Already—for whatever reason—fortune had favored him by allow-
ing circumstances in which his latent musical talent had begun to flower.
He appeared on the threshold of what promised to be a satisfying career.
Little could he have realised when, in May 1795, the British frigate, *The
Indefatigable*, docked in the Tagus to undertake repairs, that his life was
about to undergo, for the second time, a major change.

William Owen: Portrait of Sir Edward Pellew, 1st Viscount Exmouth
National Maritime Museum

2

The Indefatigable

I

In 1794 during the early years of the Revolutionary wars the success of four new French frigates cruising in the Channel was proving 'very annoying and destructive to commerce'.[1] To capitalise upon their success the French augmented their force by building six more heavy frigates, launched and equipped at Le Havre. In an attempt to counter this menace to trade, new British frigate squadrons were ordered to sea, one under the command of Sir John Borlase Warren. This new squadron of five frigates was based at Falmouth and included among its captains Sir Edward Pellew in the 38-gun *Arathusa*. Pellew was already something of a celebrity in naval circles following his capture of the French frigate *Cleopatra* off Start Point in June 1793, an action recounted in detail by William James,[2] which earned Pellew his knighthood from George III when the *Arathusa* returned to Portsmouth. Pellew, born into a distinguished and influential Cornish family in 1757, was only to serve briefly in Borlase Warren's squadron, for in 1794 he was given notice that he was to assume command of *The Indefatigable*, then refitting at Portsmouth, and to lead a second squadron of frigates, also to be based at Falmouth.

The Indefatigable had been built as a 64-gun ship-of-the-line at Buckler's Hard in 1784. Contemporary naval thought, together with the greater power of the French 74-gun fighting ships, had made her by 1794 obsolete and a major rebuild was undertaken as part of the plan of countering the threatening power of the new French frigates. The rebuild involved the removal of the original upper deck, leaving a single decked ship, a *razé*, longer, broader and much more powerful than the normal 38-gun frigates then used by the British Navy, and requiring a larger crew. James describes her as mounting

26 long 24-pounders on the main deck, and two long 12-pounders and 18
42-pound cannonades on the quarter deck and forecastle, totalling 46 guns,
with a complement of 330 men and boys.[3]

Naval terminology designated a single deck fighting ship a frigate,
however large, and so *The Indefatigable* , together with the other *razés*, was
transformed from a somewhat under-armed ship-of-the-line into an unusually large frigate.

Pellew's appointment to this powerful vessel and to his own squadron
was, in his own eyes, a vindication that both his social standing and his
naval expertise warranted a more responsible position than that which he
already held as second-in-command to Borlase Warren. On 3 February 1795
he took command of the newly refitted frigate at Portsmouth, sailing to his
Falmouth base to take up his station patrolling the Channel. On 2 May
1795 the squadron sailed for Ushant and, five days later, engaged with the
French fleet in a chase two or three miles north north west of Cape
Finisterre. *The Indefatigable* was run hard aground during the pursuit on a
submerged—and it is said, uncharted—rock, and was severely damaged.

7 May
when in Chace, the Island off Cape Finisterre, bearing SSE Easterly 2 or 3
miles, the Ship struck upon sunken rocks, before which there was no
appearance of rippling or discolour'd water, ran some Guns forward &
lower'd a boat, to sound, & in about 10 minutes, the Ship sallied deep &
started off, having 5 feet water in the Hold. Brought too for the Admiral,
people at all the Pumps, after we were off the Ship passed to Leeward of
another sunken rock, about a mile farther off Shore round which the Boat
sounded in 25 fms & the wat[er] on the Rock broke[4]

Through skilful seamanship the frigate was refloated but the damage
was too severe to be repaired at sea and, with the pumps being continuously
operated, *The Indefatigable* was ordered to Lisbon for repairs.

Pellew and his damaged frigate reached the Tagus on 10 May though
the repairs took longer than expected to complete and the ship did not sail
again until early July. Pellew's biographer, C. Northcote Parkinson, remarks
that 'the intervening period was one of great fatigue, anxiety and irrita-
tion.'[5] The frustration experienced by Pellew is caught in his log book
entries for the period. About one hundred Portuguese workmen were
employed aboard the vessel, but each action appeared to reveal further
damage; after initial cleaning and overhauling the rigging the ship had to
be moved nearer the shore for more fundamental repairs;

Friday 22 AM Unmooring the Indefatigable, & transporting her nearer the shore, riggers, caulkers, & shipwrights on board. People from the shore at the pumps...

Though some of the routine activities of the ship were maintained— Sunday services and regular reading to the crew of the Articles of War—the preliminary work appeared to have made little impression on the ship's condition.

Monday 1 June AM Shipwrights at work on board the Indefatigable people from the yard came & haul'd the Pantoon off. People from the shore still at the pumps, the ship making nearly as much water as before.

When work was commenced on the keel on 15 June it was found 'very much damaged', but eventually the work began to show progress and the frigate was prepared for sea. Pellew's frustration at this period of delay and inactivity was probably shared by the crew, and the captain records punishing several men for drunkenness and neglect of duty, rare occurrences in his logs.

On Friday 8 July the first stages were reached in preparation for going to sea.

Transported the ship to her moorings. Empd. getting the purchase ready for the Guns, Carpenters paintg the Ship's side.

It is in Lisbon during this period of enforced idleness that Joseph Emidy's life became involved with Pellew and the British Navy. The ship's muster for the period May 1–June 30[6] records one hundred supernumeraries— largely Portuguese—aboard for whom payment was being claimed for victualling. Amongst these names on the muster taken on 24 June 1795 is that of Josh. Emede[7] as number 496 of all men—regular crew, boys and supernumeraries—aboard the ship. In the following muster list for the period 1 July–30 August, the number of supernumeraries has dropped to nine. Emidy and two other men—Louis Bassel and Josh. Jacque—are now described as 'Lisbon volunteers'. Emidy was allowed 10s 10d for clothes and 2s for tobacco.

James Silk Buckingham gives the most complete surviving account of the events which determined Emidy's fate.

While thus employed [as violinist at the Lisbon opera], it happened that Sir Edward Pellew, in his frigate *The Indefatigable*, visited the Tagus, and, with some of his officers, attended the Opera. They had long wanted for the frigate a good violin player, to furnish music for the sailors' dancing in their evening leisure, a recreation highly favourable to the preservation of their good spirits and contentment. Sir Edward, observing the energy with which the young negro plied his violin in the orchestra, conceived the idea of impressing him for the service. He accordingly instructed one of his lieutenants to take two or three of the boat's crew, then waiting to convey the officers on board, and, watching the boy's exit from the theatre, to kidnap him, violin and all, and take him off to the ship. This was done, and the next day the frigate sailed: so that all hope of his escape was vain.

Surprising as it may seem, music and dancing were not uncommon features of life aboard naval vessels, even during periods of war. Other captains than Pellew also regarded dancing as a 'recreation highly favourable' to the preservation of the sailors' good spirits. In the 1750s and 1760s, as N.A.M. Rodgers' fascinating social history of the British Navy during the Seven Years War reveals,[8] some vessels maintained small bands, especially the privateers engaged in recruiting. The picture of pressed men, volunteers, and press gang joining the crew of a press tender in a dance on the hatch cover on a summer's day reveals a side of ship-board life very different from the harsher conditions endured during battles or severe weather. The crew of Admiral Hon. Edward Boscawen's flagship danced regularly in their passage across the Atlantic in 1755: the admiral, writing home to his wife, recalled how memories of the country dances they had enjoyed together in former years had been stirred by the ship's music of fiddle, fife and drum.

The importance of a violinist in contributing to the well-being of the crew is further attested to in William Bligh's log book for the ill-fated voyage of *The Bounty* as he describes enlisting the nearly blind violinist Michael Byrne.

> After 4 o'clock the evening is laid aside for their amusement and dancing. I had great difficulty before I left England to get a man to play the violin and I preferred at last to take one two-thirds blind than come without one.[9]

William Tuck, who, like Buckingham, also knew Emidy, tells a similar version of the story of the young man's capture, though he differs by locating the events off the coast of Africa:

> ... seeing his mysterious talent, [the sailors] plied him with liquor to deprive him of his senses, and while in that condition set sail for England. When this poor man recovered consciousness, he was agonised and cried piteously on finding he was stolen from his home and native land.[10]

Buckingham, a determined opponent of the slave trade, is quick to point out the essential similarities between impressment and slavery. In his description of the wretched plight of Joseph Emidy and his captivity aboard ship we perhaps catch some echoes of the young man's own feelings about his condition;

In what degree of turpitude this differed from the original stealing of the youth from his native land, and keeping him in slavery, these gallant officers, perhaps, never condescended to consider: but surely man or boy-stealing, and carrying off to forced imprisonment, is equally criminal whether it be called 'impressment' or 'slave trading.' Yet all England was roused by Clarkson, Wilberforce, and Sharpe, to protest against the African slave trade; while peers and commoners, legislators and judges, not only winked at, but gravely defended, in legislature and from the bench, the crime of man-stealing for the British navy, at the same time teaching the men thus reduced to forced servitude and imprisonment, to sing of the country that had thus enslaved them—

> The nations not so blest as thee
> Shall in their turns to tyrants fall;
> Whilst thou shalt flourish great and free,
> The dread enemy of them all.
> Rule, Britannia, Britannia rule the waves
> For Britons never shall be slaves!

Poor Emidee was thus forced, against his will, to descend from the higher regions of music in which he delighted—Gluck, Haydn, Cimarosa, and Mozart, to desecrate his violin to hornpipes, jigs, and reels, which he loathed and detested: and being, moreover, the only negro on board, he had to mess by himself, and was looked down upon as an inferior being—except when playing to the sailors, when he was of course in high favour. As the captain and officers judged, from his conduct and expressions, he was intensely disgusted with his present mode of life, and would escape at the first possible opportunity, he was never permitted to set his foot on shore for seven long years! and was only released by Sir Edward Pellew being appointed to the command of a line-of-battle-ship, L'Impetueux, when he was permitted to leave in the harbour of Falmouth, where he first landed, and remained, I believe, till the period of his death.

Though Buckingham is indignant about the method of Joseph Emidy's capture and imprisonment, the use of the press gang abroad and the taking of foreign nationals to serve on British ships was by no means uncommon. As Michael Lewis has pointed out,[11] the captain on foreign service had the responsibility to maintain his crew at full strength and to make up for the regular and heavy wastage which was the result of enemy action, sickness and death. Crew were often impressed at sea from merchant ships, privateers, smugglers and slave ships and visits to foreign ports would often be the occasion for the impressment of unwary men. The proportion of foreign nationals aboard British ships was often surprisingly high and, as an example, Lewis gives the figure of eighty foreigners out of a crew of 563 aboard *The Implacable* in 1808.[12] This total, derived from the captain's records and in no way unusual, included twenty-eight American sailors, twenty-seven from Northern Europe and a significant number from the West Indies. A survey of the records of *The Indefatigable's* crew, drawn from the muster of July and August 1797 reveals a very similar mixture of nationalities to that of *The Implacable*. The largest proportion of the 316 crew—almost seventy men—came from Cornwall and Devon; coastal regions of England from the north east to the north west were well represented and almost forty seamen originated in Scotland and thirty from Ireland. There were at least twelve American nationals aboard, as well as Swedes, Danes, Dutchmen and Norwegians and—surprisingly perhaps—a Frenchman.

Earlier in the eighteenth century some British officers, especially those engaged in the West Indies service, even kept their own slaves aboard naval ships. A liveried black youth plays a pipe and tabor to entertain three officers awaiting their meal in Hogarth's painting of Lord George Graham in his cabin, a work which probably dates from the 1740s, but the practice often had to be concealed by entering false names in the ship's muster as naval policy stressed equality for all aboard British ships; 'the laws of this country admit no badges of slavery' the Lords of the Admiralty forcibly reminded an erring Admiral in 1759.[13] Every serving man—whatever his colour or race—and regardless of whether he was a volunteer or impressed man was, in theory, treated as an equal.

One might suspect that part of Buckingham's resentment was due to the fact that Emidy was kidnapped not for an essential rôle of seamanship but for a less essential—even frivolous—occupation, but there are other instances of foreign musicians serving on a British ship. Samuel Leech in his account of his life as an ordinary seaman, *Voice from the Middle Deck*,[14] tells of a group of Italians and Spaniards who were taken on as a musical band and rated: at least, according to Leech, they were excused from fighting and flogging. Perhaps Emidy was afforded similar privileges.

II

The final preparation for *the Indefatigable's* departure from the Tagus to Falmouth took place in early July.

> Sunday 5 July at 8AM fired a gun, loosed the Foretopsail & made the Signal for a convoy.

Though painting was still being completed on the following days, the vessel moved to anchor in the fair way. On the following morning Pellew's relief at resuming his duties is apparent in his log, even though the departure was not without incident.

> Wednesday 8 July AM made the signal for the convoy to weigh with a gun, repeated the sigl. several times, ½ pas[t] 5 weigh'd & made all sail, carried away the Foretopsail yard in the slings & split the sail, got up a spare Yard & bent another sail, . . . made sail, ½ past 8 shorten'd sail & discharg'd the Pilot, half past 9 wove to the NW for the Convoy. Empd. about difft. jobs, sailors repairing the Foretopsail, at noon Convy in compy.

In the muster books after 1 September Emidy is transferred from the list of supernumeraries to the full ship's complement, being given the reference number 316 which remained with him throughout his service aboard *The Indefatigable*. A few personal details are given, recording his place of birth as Lisbon and his age at entry as 25. This detail, if accurate, would place his birth in 1770, some five years earlier than the date suggested by his grave. Neither date, however, can be documented and it is probable that Joseph Emidy himself did not know his exact age. Together with Bassel and Jacque, also 'volunteers' at Lisbon, he is described in the Qualities column of the muster which defines the status of all the rated men as LM.

This presumably signifies a *Landsman*—the lowest category of sailor, falling below Able and Ordinary Seamen. As Landsmen they would be paid at the lowest rate—16s 6d per month, as opposed to £1 2s 6d for an Able seaman and 17s 6d for an Ordinary Seaman,[15] though their duties were similar to the other ranks, including manning guns in action, daily work in the rigging and routine duties on ropes and hauling anchors. Landsmen—Emidy, Bassel and Jacque were the only men in this category on *The Indefatigable*—lacked the experience and training in seamanship though, in periods of war, were frequently required to make up deficiencies.

Their recruitment was normally by the Impress Service, often from the home port of the vessel, though, in foreign ports, the private enterprise press gang which captured Emidy and his fellow 'volunteers' would be mounted by the Captain to fill up casual vacancies in his crew. There is no way of knowing whether Bassel and Jacque were, like Emidy, musicians or whether they were pressed for other skills required by Pellew.

In addition to his pay and an allowance for 'slop cloaths' [working clothes] and tobacco, Joseph Emidy, like every sailor aboard a naval ship, would have had a standard weekly food ration issued by the Victualling Board; this included a daily pound of bread and gallon of beer and, weekly, four pounds of salt beef and two pounds of salt pork together with a regular allowance of pease, oatmeal, butter and cheese. Though plain and limited in variety, the diet was sufficient to support the heavy physical work of the seaman. Unlike many ships engaged in the foreign service where stores could run low or be affected by the climate, *The Indefatigable* was normally based close to her home port and Pellew's logs regularly record the arrival of fresh provisions. Nevertheless there must have been times when the poor quality of the food, the activities of rats or weevils, or the unexpected taking of a large number of prisoners resulted in periods of short rations.

For most of the following autumn and winter *The Indefatigable* was based at Plymouth undergoing more extensive repairs. Throughout the whole period, according to Buckingham, Emidy was held prisoner aboard.

It was during the period of repairs at Plymouth that one of the events which was further to enhance Pellew's reputation for bravery and seamanship—and incidentally to earn him new public honours, including a baronetcy—took place. In January a fierce storm drove aground the transporter ship *Dutton*, bound with a large company of soldiers for the West Indies. Plymouth harbour was not protected from westerly gales until 1812 when the breakwater was built, and a large loss of life from the *Dutton* would certainly have ensued were it not for the heroic rescue organised by Pellew.

Following her refit *The Indefatigable* spent much of the following year leading the Falmouth frigates in patrols along the French coast. Pellew's chivalry in allowing the wife of the governor of Rochefort, captured with her family in April 1796 aboard the frigate *Unité*, to return to France in a neutral ship and, in the same month, his capture of the *Virginie* without injury or loss of life amongst his crew enhanced his reputation as a commander and also enriched his purse—and that of his crew—by the prize value of the captured ships. He was also the hero of one of the most celebrated of the individual actions of the whole war in the battle with the French 74-gun *Droits de l'Homme* on the afternoon of 14 January 1797.

Ebenezer Colls: Destruction of the *Droits de l'Homme*
National Maritime Museum

This action, widely recounted and commemorated in a number of popular paintings, was unusual in that it was rare for a frigate—even a *razé* like *The Indefatigable*—to engage with a more powerful ship-of-the-line. The French ship with a crew of more than seven hundred and a large complement of soldiers was returning from the unsuccessful Irish expedition when she was encountered by the Falmouth frigates *Indefatigable* and *Amazon*. The French ship was unable to respond to the furious barrage of the English due to a violent south westerly gale; the action continued through the night until, by day break, the opposing forces were driven into Audierne bay in the face of an on-shore gale, perhaps the most dangerous weather conditions which a sailing ship could meet, let alone in a battle situation. Pellew's log[16] provides a factual, if unpunctuated, account of the action.

> Fresh breeze & hazy ¾ past noon saw a large sail made all sails in chace 10 past 4 the chace carried away her fore & main top masts we carried away the main & fore top mast . . . close reef'd top sails & stood again after the chace Amazon 7 or 8 miles a stern ¾ past 5 PM gave 3 cheers & hoisted English colours the chace hoisted french closed with her & began the action. ¾ past 6 the Amazon came up & engaged and sheered off to secure our masts & repair our rigging reengaged till 20 past 4AM when we saw land bearing NE about 2 miles . . . hauled to the wind to the southwd made night signls to the Amazon ½ past 4 last sight of the Amazon saw breakers on the lee bow went to the southwd 10 past 7 saw the enemy on her broad side without a mast & the surf breaking over her passed within a mile of her at 11 saw breakers to Leewd carried a press of sail & which enabled us to weather the Penmarks about ¾ of a mile found our ship considerable damaged in hull, mast and rigging the ship making a great deal of water

Although published some forty years later James describes the fierceness of the battle and the violence of the weather in vivid detail:

> During the whole of this long engagement, the sea ran so high, that the people on the main decks of the frigates were up to their middles in water. So violent, too, was the motion of the ships, that some of the Indefatigable's guns broke their breechings four times: some drew their ring-bolts from the side, and many of the guns, owing to the water having beaten into them, were obliged to be drawn immediately after loading . . .
>   The Indefatigable had four feet of water in the hold, and all her masts were in a wounded state. The main topmast was completely unrigged, and was saved only by uncommon alacrity.[17]

By Pellew's seamanship *the Indefatigable* escaped from the bay, though her companion, *Amazon*, was wrecked. The *Droits de l'Homme* was also wrecked, her boats crushed as they were launched, with a huge loss of life. French and English figures of the death toll differ. The French claimed 960 survivors out of a total complement of 1280 which included 580 soldiers and 50 prisoners: of the dead, 103 were killed in the frigates' attacks and the remaining 217 drowned in the wreck. The English figures for the action were higher, claiming a loss of 1350 men out of 1750. Whatever the truth, there is no doubt that Pellew's skill in commanding *The Indefatigable* avoided an even greater disaster.

Though conditions experienced in battle were horrific, these were not the greatest threat to life and limb faced by Joseph Emidy—and every other sailor—aboard ship in the late eighteenth century. Accident, foundering, wreck, fire and explosions caused greater loss of life than enemy action throughout the wars. Greater even than these was the loss of life through disease. Figures for fatal casualties in 1810 given by Lewis give some idea of the relative dangers; some 50% of casualties—2592 men in total—died as result of disease, 31% (1630) from individual accidents and 10.2% (530) from foundering, wreck or explosion, whilst enemy action claimed only 431 men, some 8.3% of the total.[18] The conditions in which the men were housed were, by modern standards appalling; worse, it was said by some, than those aboard the slave ships, for a slave who died during passage represented a loss of income to the master, and was thus a valuable commodity. This view however must be questioned, for a seaman, especially in time of war, was also a valuable commodity, and Naval regulations and practices were increasingly designed to preserve and improve the conditions in which the men lived. Considerable attention was paid to providing as balanced a diet as possible; sailors in the navy certainly fared better than those serving in merchant ships, though inevitably in long passages or in overseas service, the problems of preserving food over long periods or in hot climates could not be solved. Nevertheless, except in extreme conditions, the ordinary sailor probably ate as well, if not better, than the poor who lived ashore. Admiralty regulations were also concerned in attempting to restrict disease by improving the standards of cleanliness in the light of contemporary medical knowledge; the problem was that contemporary medical knowledge did not understand the importance of personal hygiene in inhibiting the transmission of disease. No amount of deck-scrubbing or attempts to keep as fresh as possible supply of air to the lower decks where the men lived could compensate for the cramped accommodation, persistent dampness and lack of opportunity for personal hygiene. Rats also were constant inhabitants on every ship. Though scurvy, long the enemy of the sailor, was no longer the major threat which it had been, fevers—yellow fever for those serving in hot climates and typhus resulting from the universally crowded and insanitary conditions—were by far the greatest threat to life and health experienced by seamen throughout the period.

The Indefatigable's patrols continued throughout 1797 and the following year; these were difficult years for the Navy for not only were the wars with France a major preoccupation but unrest among the English seamen themselves caused growing concern amongst the senior officers. Though the Falmouth squadrons were not directly affected by the mutiny of the Fleet at Spithead in April 1797, conditions were not good and there was always concern that the unrest might spread.

The latter part of 1797 did not rival in danger the action with the *Droits de l'Homme* in January. The ship's log[19] records patrols off Ushant, though much of the summer months were spent moored in the Carrick Roads and in Torbay. The autumn saw periods of action at more westerly locations, moving from the Scillies to Madiera, Palma and Tenerife before reaching a position off the port of Lisbon, the only recorded occasion when Joseph Emidy returned close to his erstwhile home.

> Tuesday 24 October. Off Port of Lisbon
> Strong gales of wind . . . saw a strange sail in the SE gave chace at 11 . . . the chace a Brig from Boston bound to Lisbon at 12 gave chace to a sail in the NW

Pellew's opportunist pursuit of passing ships was to prove more successful on the following day:

> Wednesday 25 October
> . . . fired several shot at the chace at 5PM She fired a gun & hoisted french colours at ½p[ast].

The vessel proved to be the 'Hienna Privateer from Bayonne' with two hundred and twenty two men aboard, and she was duly captured by *The Indefatigable*. Pellew and his prize returned to Falmouth, a journey which lasted until 15 November when the ships moored in the Carrick Roads. On that day almost two hundred and fifty prisoners were 'discharged to Falmo. Prison'.[20] The movement of such a large company of prisoners caused inevitable problems in the town, as John Skinner records in his journal of his Cornish journey.

> November 15: Falmouth
> Mounting our horses at twelve, we proceeded on the road to Truro, but were

detained upwards of an hour, just as we were leaving the Town by observing some French prisoners landed, they were two hundred and eighty in number, they were taken in two ships, the one a Corvette, and the other a Brig, by Sir Edwards Pellew ... I could not but remark that the Officers had not the least appearance of gentlemen, and several as they had been mostly risen from the mast.[21]

The winter of 1797 and much of 1798 was more peacefully spent in making a survey of St. Mary's Road, Scilly, investigating its potential as an anchorage for the Channel Fleet to use as a base for watching Brest and defending Ireland. Judging from the brief entries in his log and the apparent haste with which they were compiled, it was not a period of great interest to the energetic and adventure-seeking Pellew. There were few chases with the opportunity for action and prize money. The transportation of men from a Chatham hospital ship in early April 1798, the pursuit of a French Brig sailing from Bordeaux and an encounter with a Brig sailing from Stockholm with news of the French fleet were the only events which gave spice to routine activities.

On 1 March 1799 Pellew's command was transferred from *Indefatigable* to *L'Impetueux*, a prize of the 'Glorious First of June' battle of 1794 and now sailing under the British flag. It is clear that he did not relish the change and move to Portsmouth. At Falmouth, as a major property owner and a prominent member of local society, as well as being in command of his own detachment, Pellew had an independence which the Portsmouth appointment did not offer. There he was to be in command of a line-of-battle ship, under the direct control of an admiral, and he was unwilling to forgo his present position for a lessening of responsibilities. His protests were not successful and he was unable to resist the move to Portsmouth and his new ship.

It was at this period that Pellew allowed Emidy to go ashore as a free man after a period of almost five years at sea; Buckingham claims seven years, but this does not accord with the facts.

The change of command in a naval ship was always the occasion for a major reorganisation of the crew. Many men would choose to follow a successful captain—and success could be measured not only in popularity but in the frequency and amount of 'prize money' which the captain earned—to his new post. A number of such postings were recorded in the 'Reason for Discharge' column in the muster entries for 1 January–28 February 1799[22] when the name of Pellew's new command, *L'Impetueux*, appears. Amongst such entries is the name of Joseph Emidy, discharged from *The Indefatigable* on 28 February. As Buckingham tells us that Emidy informed him that Pellew allowed the young man his freedom at this point, it was probably simpler, considering the nature of his 'volunteering' for the navy, to record his discharge as a transfer of posting rather than give the real reason. Joseph Jacque who entered the service at Lisbon at the same time as Emidy remained in *The Indefatigable's* company under the new captain.

Allowances paid to Joseph Emidy in the muster throughout his service had varied, reaching a maximum of £2 11s 10d for 'slop cloathes' in September 1796, but falling to 5s between May 1797 and early 1798. £1 10s was allowed as 'wages remitted from abroad' on two occasions in 1798 and, in the month of his discharge Emidy was allowed 11s. for 'slop cloathes' and 11s. for tobacco. Seamen's wages were often paid at the end of a period of service and would amount to a considerable sum of accumulated back pay. No record has been traced of such payments to Emidy.

One can only speculate on the emotions of the young man in his mid twenties as he spent his first days in the country which was to become his home for the remainder of his life. Having experienced such dangerous actions aboard *The Indefatigable* the relief which he felt must have been counteracted by the very unfamiliarity of the surroundings. Though the sights and sounds of Falmouth harbour cannot have been unfamiliar, and the outline of the Cornish coast seen from the sea must have become known to him, it is still difficult to comprehend the nature of his feelings as he prepared to enter—yet again—a new pattern of life.

PART TWO

Cornwall 1799–1835

View of Falmouth & Sr I. Borlase Warren's Prizes entering the Harbour.

Nicholas Pocock: Falmouth Harbour

Borlase Warren was Pellew's rival commander of a company of frigates at Falmouth; the scene of his frigates and prize ships was engraved by Pocock the year after Joseph Emidy was discharged at the port.

Royal Institution of Cornwall

3

A New Life: Falmouth

I

The Falmouth in which Joseph Emidy was turned ashore in 1799 was probably little different from the town which offered so limited entertainment to William Beckford twelve years earlier. The military and naval presence had grown since the 1780s and the character of a bustling sea port preoccupied predominantly with the activities of war and the packet boats might not have seemed the best place for a foreigner to try to earn a living. In one sense, however, Joseph Emidy may have been fortunate in that the nature of the community with its constantly changing personalities, moving in and out of the town as their duties demanded, must have made it rather easier to integrate as a stranger than if he had been abandoned in a town less accustomed to a migrant population. In another sense also the nature of the changing society meant that there was a continued search for diversions and entertainments; musical accomplishments were highly regarded as a social attribute by both young men and women, and a gifted teacher of popular instruments could probably find work both among the local community and among the families of naval and army personnel stationed in the area. Teaching a wide variety of instruments became a prominent feature of Emidy's work fairly quickly and it probably provided the basis of his livelihood for the remainder of his life for, in all the advertisements for concerts which he later promoted, his teaching activities are prominently mentioned. One can only speculate how remunerative this work proved to be, as evidence of tuition fees expected by music teachers is very rare. In 1813, Christiana, a 'professor' of pianoforte and singing in Truro and Penryn advertised three lessons a fortnight to residents of the towns for an annual fee of eight guineas, together with an enrolment fee of one guinea.[1] This is a not inconsiderable sum, though a successful teacher would need quite a large group of pupils to provide a comfortable living.

James Silk Buckingham's account suggests that there was a scarcity of music teachers in Falmouth and we may assume that Emidy as 'the only teacher procurable . . . who taught equally well the piano, violoncello, clarinet and flute' probably found a ready supply of pupils. Early advertisements add the guitar and mandolin to his list of accomplishments, stressing that he taught them 'in a most easy and elegant stile'.[2] His activities as a music teacher probably allowed him to integrate into the social order of the community more effectively than almost any other profession which he could have followed; it also brought him into contact with many musical amateurs who promoted concerts and organised the amateur orchestras—the Harmonic societies—which were a popular feature of music making in the early nineteenth century. These societies—and there was one in most Cornish towns of any size—frequently employed professional players, if any were available, to strengthen their public performances and, as Emidy's name and reputation spread, we find him increasingly involved throughout much of the county in this capacity.

No doubt his unusual ability as a violinist proved a valuable advertisement to all who heard him. Buckingham describes him playing 'to a degree of perfection never before heard in Cornwall' and William Tuck reinforces and expands this opinion;

> This remarkable man was the most finished musician I ever heard of, though I have had the privilege of listening to most of the stars who have appeared on the London stage during the past fifty years, but not one of them in my estimation has equalled this unknown Negro. He was not only a wonderful manipulator on the violin, 'cello, or viola, but could write fluently in either of these clefs; his hands seemed especially adapted for the work, his extremely long, thin fingers were not much larger than a goose quill: where this great talent came from was always a mystery to me, and to all who came in contact with him.[3]

Teaching, balls and concerts provided Joseph Emidy with his principal sources of income, though the peripatetic nature of the work with its hard physical demands of travelling from town to town and the inevitably modest standards of most of his fellow performers must have seemed a different reality from the prospects which were beginning to open for him during the Lisbon years; an advertisement from the *West Briton* of 1 December 1820—typical of many—gives an indication of the range of work which grew from the early teaching contacts in Falmouth;

> Violin, Tenor, Bass-Viol, Guitar, and Spanish Guitar, taught as usual; Balls and Assemblies attended; Harps tuned, and Piano-Fortes buffed, regulated

and tuned, according to the directions of Messrs. BROADWOOD and SONS, in any part of the County.

Emidy's integration into the community was further advanced by his marriage: though he was 'one of the very ugliest negroes' that Buckingham had ever seen, he 'had charms enough to fascinate a young white woman of a respectable tradesman's family.' The marriage of Joseph Emedy [sic] and Jenefer [sic] Hutchins is recorded in the register of Falmouth Parish Church on 16 September, 1802. The same register was to record—with varying spellings—the births, baptisms and, once, death of their children over the next ten years. Joseph, the eldest son of Joseph and Jane [sic], was born on 23 July 1803 and baptised on 14 August. Thomas Hutchins, 6 July 1805 [baptised 8 December], James Hutchings [sic], 13 July 1808 [baptised 11 March 1809], Cecilia Hutchins—their only daughter—21 October 1809 [baptised 10 June 1810]. The last Falmouth entry for the family records the death on 3 August 1812 of an infant, Benjamin, born on 24 June 1812 and baptised four days before his death. Some time after the death of Benjamin the family moved to Truro where a further son, Richard, was born. Richard was only to survive his father by two years, dying in his mid-twenties in 1837. The obituary notice of Richard Emidy commended his devotion as a Sunday school teacher, which may be an indication that the Emidy family took religious devotions seriously. Thomas in later life was to combine the professions of cabinet maker and carpenter as well as following his father's musical interests as leader of a Quadrille Band. Joseph, however, may have proved a troublesome member of the family for in 1816, aged twelve, he appeared before the Cornwall Easter sessions for 'stealing a quantity of pence, from the shop of Elizabeth John, who resides in St. Clements Street, Truro'. The youth confessed to stealing about fifteen shillings and, although ten shillings was recovered, he received a sentence of six months hard labour.

II

It was with the amateur orchestral society in Falmouth that Joseph Emidy began to rebuild his career as a performer. The activities of the Harmonic Society as, like similar groups throughout England, the Falmouth musicians called themselves, are remarkably difficult to chronicle. Most of the players, the 'Gentlemen Amateurs' as they are invariably called, were drawn from the better educated members of society. They met regularly—often fortnightly or monthly—in private houses or, occasionally, public rooms. Most of the meetings were private and were never advertised. Occasionally the societies gave concerts which were advertised and received notices in the local press, but this practice was by no means common. The activities were primarily designed for the self-improvement and entertainment of the members. Many societies drew upon the services of local professional musicians, when available, and, quite clearly, the arrival of a performer of the calibre of Joseph Emidy would have been welcomed; as Buckingham recalls;

> he first began by going out to parties to play the violin, which he did to a degree of perfection never before heard in Cornwall; this led to his being engaged as a teacher, and then a leader at concerts; so that by degrees, he made rapid progress in reputation and means.

The financial conditions behind such arrangements are not clear, but one method which several Harmonic societies used to reimburse their professional colleagues was by promoting a concert—often annually—for the benefit of the leader. A number of such events for Emidy and other musicians can be traced in various towns throughout the first decades of the century. Normally these concerts, which often concluded with a ball, were the only events which were advertised and reported in the press for a higher monetary return was expected; the regular meetings usually passed unrecorded. Nevertheless it is possible from memoirs and other passing references to piece together some account—albeit incomplete—of the personalities and tastes of these societies.

Buckingham, it will be recalled, first came into contact with Emidy when he decided to take up the flute to bring him into contact with young ladies; his musical progress was swift enough to allow him to play the solo part in a concerto by Hoffmeister

> with great *eclat* in one of the monthly concerts of the Harmonic Society of Falmouth, held at the Town Hall, where Emidee was the leader, Major Wall, of the Wiltshire Militia, then in garrison at Pendennis Castle, playing the first violin: Mr Jordan, Deputy Collector of Customs, the tenor [viola]; Mr Lott, of the Post Office, second flute; and the rest of the orchestra made up of the militia band and amateurs.

As the novels of Jane Austen show in reflecting the atmosphere of the age, the presence of a garrison or the visit of a company of soldiers had an enormous impact upon society in small towns and rural areas. During 1806 the Truro assembly was on more than one occasion 'enlivened by the presence of several naval and marine officers' who did much to remedy the 'disproportion of ladies'[4] and many other events up and down the county record the attendance of a military band as well as the officers of a visiting regiment. The musical contribution of these visitors was usually, but not invariably, appreciated; the Rev. John Skinner's visit to the Bodmin assembly in 1797 was one such occasion when opinion was divided.

> This is a monthly meeting for which the charge is a moderate subscription of 5s. for the season, though the entertainment to be sure does not discredit this vast expense. The room they dance in is perhaps twenty five feet long, the boards laid the contrary way, and some of them much higher than others, which occasions various trippings as you go down the dance. It is lighted by five or six candles stuck against the wall, and the music usually consists of a blind fiddler and a little scraper, his son. But we were particularly fortunate on the occasion of our visit in having the band of the Somerset Militia, who not only occupied half the room, but stunned us with the noise of their drums, clarionettes, etc.. Indeed, I should have been much better pleased if Mr Fiddler had reigned alone. The ladies, however, seemed perfectly charmed and contented, and I was accordingly glad to get away before tea, leaving them to the society of the Red Coats.[5]

Though the British army had long employed musicians to undertake specific duties, leading the marching and conveying messages through fanfares, formalised regimental bands, emulating similar establishments in Germany, date from the middle of the eighteenth century. In 1762 the Royal Artillery raised a 'band of music', blending brass and woodwind instruments which established the pattern which was to be copied by other regiments; the Royal Artillery Band consisted of pairs of trumpets, horns and bassoons and four instrumentalists who doubled on clarinets and oboes. In many regiments the bands were maintained unofficially at the officers' expense and inevitably remained small throughout the second half of the century. In the larger regiments the bands began to grow at the turn of the century, largely by increasing the number of clarinets and by adding flutes, or fifes, but the characteristic blend of wind and brass remained the distinctive feature. Brass bands did not begin to develop until the 1830s; though some cavalry regimental bands had traditionally favoured brass instruments, largely trumpets supported by drums, the musical usefulness of the brass ensemble was severely limited by the nature of the instruments themselves; the natural trumpet could only play a limited number of notes, determined by the harmonic series. Whilst this limitation was appropriate for fanfares and other military signals, more sophisticated melodies were impossible and, until the invention of the keyed bugle and, later, the valved cornet, brass bands had no real potential for musical development. The limitations of the brass instruments were of course no real problem in the military bands; the clarinets or oboes with their increasingly elaborate key systems replacing the complex cross-fingering of their keyless predecessors, could deal with any melodic complexity.

The growth of the volunteer regiments in the later years of the century saw a further spread of military bands. Though these bands rarely matched in size those of the established regiments, they retained a similar balance of instruments; many small bands would consists of two clarinets, or oboes, two horns and bassoons with a trumpet and, occasionally, a serpent. The repertory of regimental and militia bands tended to be based upon marches and quicksteps, often composed by the local bandmasters, but occasionally the work of established musicians; Haydn, for example, wrote marches for this combination of instruments during his first London visit in 1791–1792. Though the bands primary purpose may have originally been purely military, their function was beginning to change; the arrival of the regiment in a town or village with band playing and drums beating must have brought to many small communities a sense of excitement and occasion rarely experienced. No doubt the atmosphere created was a powerful stimulus to recruiting drives as the regiments, permanent and volunteer, strove to generate the patriotic zeal which encouraged young men to join the colours. Though musicians were often employed aboard naval vessels, it is significant that many navy recruiting companies usually employed a band for similar purposes. The participation of the militia in town and national ceremonies, such as the Royal birthday celebrations and election meetings, must also have given a sense of ceremony rare in daily life. The officers were also quick to recognise the value of the band in providing social music for dances and balls in which the militia's involvement in the local community was stressed. Outside church and chapel, formal music making of any sort can only have been a rare experience for many people in the late eighteenth and early nineteenth centuries. Concert going was an experience which only the more affluent could enjoy; for the majority, the militia bands, small as they were, provided a glimpse of the pleasures which music could offer.

Falmouth audiences had the luxury of military or naval musicians almost permanently in the town to complement local resources. Concerts and balls were rarely presented without a band in attendance. The first musical event to be advertised in the new *Royal Cornwall Gazette* [10 October 1801] sets a pattern which was to be followed over the next quarter century.

Concert and Ball

Mr Holland respectfully informs the Ladies and Gentlemen of Falmouth, Penryn, and their vicinity, that on Friday evening the 16th instant, will be performed at Wynn's Hotel, a grand Miscellaneous CONCERT, by the Band of the Royal Cornwall Militia, assisted by the Gentlemen of the Falmouth Harmonic Society, First Violin by Mr.ABBOT; Vocal Part and Principal Clarinet by Mr. HOLLAND. After the Concert will be a BALL.

Militia bands were also introduced into the theatre; in a report on the performance given in Falmouth by 'Signior [sic] Saxoni . . . the First Rope Dancer in the World' the *Gazette* contributor wrote:

We congratulate the manager on the respectable augmentation that has taken place in the orchestra by the assistance of several of the musicians in the North Devon band, whose masterly skill and execution cannot fail of contributing much to the amusement of the audience.[6]

Mr. Holland extended his activities with the Royal Cornwall Band by presenting a concert in Penryn early in January 1802.[7] In July of the same year Joseph Emidy placed a series of advertisements for a 'Grand MISC-ELLANEOUS CONCERT' to be held at Wynn's Hotel on 19 August.[8] This is the first appearance of his name in the newspaper and the unusually detailed entry suggests that this was the first of the concerts to be presented for his benefit. The concert was to include symphonies by Stamitz, overtures by Eichner and Martini, guitar and mandolin solos performed by Emidy, and was to conclude with a fully choral version of the National Anthem. The centre piece was a Violin Concerto composed and performed by Emidy himself. The former slave and reluctant sailor was revealing another unexpected talent!

Within a year or two he was also widening his contacts; on 7 April 1804 the *Royal Cornwall Gazette* announced a Concert and Ball at Truro.

Joseph Emidy humbly begs leave to inform the Ladies and Gentlemen of this Neighbourhood, that the Gentlemen of the Truro Subscription Concert have condescended to honor him by their assistance at a Grand Miscellaneous Concert . . .

The programme for the concert to be held during the Sessions week was less detailed than that given for Falmouth though certain items—the guitar and mandolin solos and the national anthem—recur. It may well have already appeared to Emidy that Truro was more likely to prove the best centre for a successful musical career and the town gradually overtook

Falmouth as the centre for most of Emidy's concerts even before he took the step of moving home and family. He did however promote one more event in his first Cornish home. In 1806 he advertised a concert at Mrs Hick's School Room, 'honoured with the assistance of several Gentlemen performers, and the Band of the North Devon Militia'. On this occasion, unlike his first concert, there were no details of the programme, though vocal and instrumental music was promised. Tickets cost three shillings and six pence and were available from the musician's home 'near the market place in Falmouth'.[9]

Though the reasons for it are not clear, the activities of the Falmouth Harmonic Society fell into decline. Concerts were no longer advertised and, though members may have continued to meet privately, no evidence remains. A similar decline is apparent in the success of the theatre company based in the town. Not until 1819 is there any further reference to the orchestral society when a concert is postponed in Truro to 'avoid interfering with the Concerts at Falmouth'.[10] A move to reform the society was made in 1824 and, once again, the old partiality for wind bands was in evidence.

> Philharmonic societies have been formed at Falmouth under the direction of Messrs. Wynn and Hervey, and at Helston, under the management of Messrs. Pascoe and Drew; the latter are similar to those in this town [Truro], but the Falmouth amateurs prefer the martial sounds of the instruments generally heard in a military band, none of the *fiddle* kind being admitted.[11]

Selections from Mozart, Rossini and Beethoven were included in a successful concert which attracted more than two hundred listeners in January 1825.

> The company expressed the highest gratification at the performance and the taste and judgement displayed by the conductor [Mr. Webb]. The ball commenced immediately after the concert had concluded—about fifty couples were engaged in this exhilarating exercise, which was continued with great spirit to a late, or rather, an *early* hour.[12]

In spite of the audience's preference for military bands, the Falmouth amateurs gave occasional concerts which included strings,[13] and a monthly season was re-established. Sporadic activity in Falmouth was reported in the following seasons, but it would appear that the most exciting years had passed. The concert reported in the *Royal Cornwall Gazette* on 12 March 1825 must have been a melancholy affair; the amateurs of the Harmonic Society combined with 'as many members of the band of the 31st. regiment as survived the unfortunate loss of the Kent', and the event of April 1828 to celebrate the birthday of George IV appears to have been subservient to the Ball which followed.

The 'bill of fare' ... includes some novelties, with the standard vocal and instrumental pieces of the best authors, and has not the common fault of being too lengthy as to become tedious, particularly as the Concert is to be succeeded by a Ball.[14]

4

A 'display of Beauty, Rank and Fashion': Cornwall's First Music Festivals

I

In the early years of the nineteenth century more ambitious plans to enrich the Cornish musical and social scene were afoot. An abortive attempt to focus interest in an elaborate festival of music appears to have taken place in 1802. The *Cornwall Gazette* of 18 September reports:

> Preparations are making here for a grand musical festival to be performed in the truly beautiful church of Truro. If we are rightly informed the preparations are such as augur a high treat to the *amateurs* in that divine science. It is intended for the benefit of the Cornwall Infirmary, an institution of the utmost public utility, which reflects the highest honor on its patrons and the county. It will be no proof of taste or liberality not to be present at this solemn festival.

Nothing seems to have come from this proposal and four years later the paper, now dignified by its *Royal* epithet and published in Truro instead of Falmouth, printed a similar announcement for a 'grand oratorio at Truro, in the course of the ensuing summer'.[1] The proceeds were destined once more for the Cornwall Infirmary which had been opened in 1799.

Plans were further advanced than when the paper had printed its announcement four years earlier, since seven weeks later on 31 May it was able to give more definite details to whet the appetite of its readers.

> The approaching musical festival at Truro promises to be one of the most attractive entertainments ever enjoyed in this county. Something of the kind, we believe, was once given in the neighbourhood of Penzance; but for that

place, with all its natural attractions, is too remote from the central and eastern parts of Cornwall, to become a general rendezvous of all the beauty, fashion, and respectability of the county: Truro is the most central, as well as the largest town in Cornwall. This exquisite treat is to begin in September, when all the first rate London singers and performers are engaged for a grand oratorio at Taunton, another at Plymouth, and to terminate their tour at Truro.

This account continues by stressing the worth and respectability of the promoters and promises that 'the novel assemblage of equipages, dashing beaux, and blooming belles . . . will altogether combine in a jubilee more delightful than has ever been witnessed in this part of the kingdom'.

Throughout June, July and August further information was gradually released. The list of stewards, printed on 19 July, included most of the local gentry and parliamentary representatives; the managing steward was named as Richard Taunton M.D. Dr. Taunton, physician to the Cornwall Infirmary from 1808,[2] was a fine example of the breadth of interest which characterised the early nineteenth-century educated gentleman. In addition to his professional duties, he assembled in manuscript much information about the history of Truro, basing his information not only upon documentary sources but on the memories of the older inhabitants of the town. His lectures on acoustics to the Cornwall Literary and Philosophical Institution drew 'repeated thunders of applause'[3] and he may even have been the performer on the double bass in the first subscription concert to be held in Lostwithiel in 1816 whose contribution to the concert was much admired.[4] Moreover, as managing steward for the festival in 1806, much of the day-to-day administration and ultimate responsibility for the success of this complex venture must have fallen to his lot.

In the weeks preceding the festival the search for accommodation became intense and hectic; private parties gathered from all over the county, lists of vacant accommodation for visitors—and their horses—were displayed at the *Royal Cornwall Gazette* Office and there was eager anticipation throughout the town:

> . . . in short 'all the world' is to be here; every room in the town will be crowded, and 'three in a bed' will be deemed comfortable lodging. The very fleas in the Barracks tremble for their quarters; while cat gut, perfumer, and *doctor-bunnies* have risen already fifty per cent!—Then 'hey to the Jubilee'.[5]

The gathering of nobility and especially of officialdom caused suspicion and apprehension in humbler minds:

A penurious old farmer in the neighbourhood of St. Columb, in whose mind
the burthen of taxes is ever uppermost, upon reading the list of Stewards,
the major part of whom are Senators, and associating their names with the
music, exclaimed, 'What! now the *Pearlament men* have shut up their house,
they are coming to *sing* the money out of folks pockets, are they?'[6]

The meeting of the leaders of society however had significant benefits
for the sporting fraternity for, during the course of the festival, opportunity
was taken to hold discussions which resulted in the revival of Bodmin races
in the following year.[7]

The cause of the excitement—at least among those with a genuine interest
in music—was the number and calibre of the visiting performers. Such a
range and quality had not appeared before in Cornwall. The managing
directors were the Ashley brothers, 'Managers of the Oratorios at the
Theatre Royal, Covent Garden'. The Ashley family—John Ashley and his
four instrumentalist sons—had been closely associated with the musical
activities of the capital for many years and had been active in organising
and promoting provincial music festivals. The younger members of the
family led the sections of the orchestra and prominent singers from the
London theatres, supported by choral singers from the Ancient Concerts
and boys from the Chapel Royal, provided the vocal contributions. John
Ashley, assistant to John Bates in the first Handel Commemoration Festival
of 1784 and, from 1795, manager of the Lenten season of oratorios at Covent
Garden, had died in 1805 but his sons continued his performing and
promoting activities. Three sons were involved in the tour of the west as
leader, organist and principal 'cellist. A nucleus of visiting professional
instrumentalists formed the orchestra and the Ashleys' requirements were
supplemented by the 'most approved Performers', local gentlemen amateurs and professional players. A similar manner of recruitment was
adopted for the chorus and altogether 'fifty at instruments and thirty
choristers' were expected.[8] The necessity to import the chorus as well as
the instrumentalists indicates that the great choral tradition which was to
become such a dominant feature of English musical life later in the century
was not yet in evidence. Some years later if any impresario had proposed
to import a chorus it would have been regarded not simply as an
extravagant 'coals to Newcastle' undertaking but—more seriously—as a
slight upon the musical achievements of his hosts. The first signs of amateur
choral societies promoting concerts, as opposed to singing in church
services, do not occur until the 1820s when the St. Austell Parish Church
choir under Bennett Swaffield gave occasional recitals.

Though the orchestra must have been the most complete and capable, the chorus the most experienced, which many of the audience had encountered, the principal attraction was without doubt the star vocalists. The activities of the *prima donnas* of the London stage, their professional rivalry and their cultivation of the current taste for ornamenting the music with florid decoration were familiar to provincial audiences from accounts in popular journals and from eyewitness reports by those returning from London and Bath. The 1806 Festival brought to Cornwall not one but two of these star singers, supported by three leading male vocalists. Signiora Griglietti had made her London debut earlier in the year in *La Clemenza di Tito*, the first production of a Mozart opera in England. Her performance had been well received and she was a rising star to be watched. The chief attraction however was Mrs. Dickons who had made her reputation as a notable Polly in *The Beggar's Opera* in the 1790s and consolidated her fame to become a favourite of English audiences for more than twenty years. In particular Mrs. Dickons was a focal point for the admiration and support of those who preferred native singers to the foreign artists who periodically captivated the fashionable audiences.[9]

Sadly the printed handbills on which detailed programmes were announced do not appear to have survived but general arrangements for the six concerts in Truro were printed in the paper. Three sacred concerts were held at eleven o'clock in St. Mary's Church on Tuesday 9 September, and the following Wednesday and Friday; the Wednesday performance of *Messiah* in the version which Mozart had added accompaniments to Handel's original orchestration bringing it into line with the orchestral style, taste and fashion of the late eighteenth century. At eight o'clock each evening a 'Grand Miscellaneous Concert' was to be held in the Theatre including 'Symphonies, Songs, Solos, and Concertos, by most of the principal performers; and some of the most favorite Glees'. Admission to a theatre box and to the church cost seven shillings, whilst the gallery in the theatre cost three shillings and six pence. All the performers were requested to attend a rehearsal at the church on Monday morning before the festival commenced.

'The proud little capital' wrote an anonymous writer in a letter, supposedly found in the road near the Post Office and printed in the *Royal Cornwall Gazette* of 20 September, 'was all in a bustle of preparation'. The roads were filled 'with country psalm-singers, blind fiddlers &.&.' and 'carriages . . . among which were some very handsome coaches and four with coronets, &., began to roll in grand curves through the spacious streets and beautiful oblong square of the market place.' The festival, however, nearly failed before it commenced; at the hour set for rehearsal on Monday

... the whole musical corps was lost ... they had embarked at Plymouth for
an aquatic journey to Truro: but the elements now-a-days are music
proof—they were driven into Fowey ... and arrived in Truro just in time to
dissipate the clouds of anticipated disappointment.

According to the anonymous correspondent Wednesday's *Messiah* was
the highlight, drawing into the audience a wide cross section of society,
the fashionable listener as well as the 'honest sun-burnt faces of humble
life'.

While the pearly drop still trembled in many a brilliant eye, in an adjoining
pew might be seen an honest tinner, quelling the tumult which a forced
march of twelve miles before breakfast had raised in his stomach, by a
vigorous appeal to his pasty; a little further on, on your left, you behold a
poor old woman striving to restore peace to her shattered nerves, by a suck
of gin from a thumb-bottle.

This is an astonishing, if romanticised, testimony to the appeal of *Messiah*
in transcending social and musical barriers; it is unlikely that the 'honest
tinner' would have ventured into the Theatre for one of the concerts, though
the spiritual and musical qualities of Handel's work exercised a powerful
hold on the imagination throughout the country.

Fashionable society was more in evidence at the evening concerts; the
audience 'exceeded in elegance the morning display at the church' and was
'more distinctly classed'. The performances were enthusiastically received.

The amateurs were in ecstasies ... and as 'music is the food of love', beaux
of three score, throwing aside the lumber of years, might be seen trembling
to touch Griglietti's garment.

In the light of this lively account it is not surprising that the final report
of the festival, printed on 25 October, remarks that 'no other town in the
Messrs. Ashley's musical tour answered their expectations so well as Truro'.
Financially the concert for the benefit of the Cornwall Infirmary realised
more than £60[10] and, three years later the *Royal Cornwall Gazette* recorded
that more than seven hundred guineas had been taken for tickets sold in
their office alone.[11]

The most complete account of the concerts themselves appeared on 13
September 1806. This itemises a number of pieces which had not been
included in the advertisements and captures something of the variety and
vitality of the performances; the displays of virtuosity, both in rapidity of
execution and in range of ornamentation introduced to delight and astonish

the audience, call for particular comment, as does the unique—and at the time unfamiliar—qualities of the counter-tenor voice.

The several concertos by Messrs. Ashley, Griesbach, Holmes and Hyde, on the violin, violoncello, hautboy, bassoon and trumpet, were performed in the most finished stile and rapid execution: that on the violoncello by Mr. Charles Ashley was particularly applauded, more especially the air of 'Auld Robin Gray' which he played with the double stop. Signora Griglietti possesses much more fullness of voice than we were led to expect: she sang with great sweetness, and was particularly successful in the song 'With Verdure Clad' from Haydn's 'Creation'. Mr. Doyle possesses considerable power of voice, but amongst all his songs 'The Wolf' by Shield, excited the most applause. Mr. Vaughan's sweet tenor voice can never fail of being highly pleasing, and Mr. Goss's fine contr'alto was exceedingly admired by the dilettante, and both pleased and astonished those who were unaccustomed to that tone and compass. But 'though last not least', Mrs. Dickons was received . . . with reiterated bursts of applause. All her songs were so well sung that it is difficult which most to admire, whether the touching pathos of her plaintive tones, the full mellowness of her swell, the execution of her *bravura*, or the sprightliness of her allegro: in short,for compass of voice and true taste, it will be long before we shall 'look upon her like again'. To sum up the whole, the selection, the performance, and the support which the managers have received from the stewards and the public, have so satisfied all parties that it has been proposed and unanimously carried and accepted, to renew this festival triennially.

II

After the excitement of the 1806 Festival Cornish musical life reverted to its accustomed sporadic existence. Occasional visitors enlivened the scene with brief tours of the county, publicised and reported in the paper. Mademoiselle Merelle entertained on the harp at Truro Theatre 'from the compositions of Kozeluch, Mozart, Haydn, Dussek and others' in September 1806, and the seven-year-old keyboard prodigy, Miss Randles, appeared both in Truro and Falmouth during April 1807. Other entertaining visitors included Mr. Clarke with his 'AEthereal, Philosophical and Chemical Fire Works' in February 1807 and Mr. Bannister's 'Divertisement' of popular songs, recitations and sketches. The most important musical event was the return to his native county for his first professional visit of the singer Charles Incledon.

Incledon, the son of an apothecary and surgeon, had been born in 1763 at St. Keverne. At the age of eight he joined the choir of Exeter Cathedral where he was a pupil of William Jackson, the distinguished organist and composer, winning local fame as a boy soprano. Following an engagement aboard *The Thunderer* in Torbay, Incledon resolved to go to sea to follow a naval career. He joined the service in 1779 probably after the breaking of his voice and eventually joined the *Raisonnable* under the command of Lord Hervey. He continued to sing during his naval service, and as his mature tenor voice developed, he impressed senior naval figures, including Admiral Pigot, commander of the fleet, who frequently sent for Incledon to join him and Admiral Hughes in performing glees and catches. Such interest and patronage proved valuable when he returned to England in 1783 and decided to follow a musical career on the stage. Admiral Pigot and Lord Hervey were amongst those who gave letters of introduction to Sheridan and Coleman supporting Incledon's aspirations. Though he initially failed to gain employment in London, he was engaged at Southampton in 1784 and—more importantly—at Bath in the following year. The musical scene at Bath was second only to that of London and the presiding arbiter of musical taste was the Italian castrato, composer and teacher, Venanzio Rauzzini. Born in 1746, Rauzzini had sung leading operatic roles throughout Europe, including the first performances of a number of works by the young Mozart, before settling in London, and later Bath, in 1774; his career as a performer was now secondary to his work as a composer and teacher. In the latter capacity his pupils included almost every leading British singer of the age including Nancy Storace, Michael Kelly, who were both to appear in the first performance of *Le Nozze di Figaro*, Braham and Mrs. Billington. Incledon attracted the attention of Rauzzini who gave him lessons and introduced him at concerts. In 1786 Incledon obtained an engagement at Vauxhall Gardens and for the next few years he divided his year between the summer at Vauxhall and the winter at Bath. In 1790 he was engaged at Covent Garden, establishing a reputation as one of the leading tenors of his day, gaining particular claim for his performance of Macheath in Gay's *The Beggar's Opera*; he also performed in provincial festivals and the Lenten oratorios, and, after 1804, he created a popular entertainment, 'The Wandering Melodist', which featured nautical and patriotic ballads.

The concert platform may have suited his abilities better than the stage, for, though admired for the excellence of his voice, his acting was regarded as clumsy and wooden, and his musicianship and intelligence were judged as not being of the highest order. William Parke writing his memoirs in 1830 attributed these defects to Incledon's character which was made up of 'a singular compound of contrarieties, amongst which frugality and extravagance were conspicuous'.[12] Leigh Hunt expressed a similar view more forcibly;

> It is a pity I cannot put upon paper the singular gabblings of that actor, the lax and sailor-like twist of mind, with which everything hung upon him, and his profane pieties in quoting the Bible; for which, and swearing, he seemed to have an equal reverence.[13]

There were few who questioned the beauty of Incledon's voice however, and his particular ability to merge the lower tones of the chest voice with a higher *falsetto* register; this gift may have been natural though the experience of studying with Rauzzini can only have developed the singer's ability to conceal the break in his vocal register. As the *Musical Quarterly* wrote in 1818:

> He had a voice of uncommon power, both in the natural and falsetto. The former was from A to G, a compass of about fourteen notes; the latter he could use from D to E or F, or about ten notes . . . His falsetto was rich, sweet and brilliant, but totally unlike the other. He took it without preparation, according to circumstances, either about D, E, or F, or ascending an octave, which was his most frequent custom.[14]

In 1808 Incledon was in dispute with the theatre management, and engaged in a lengthy provincial tour which brought him to several Cornish towns in December. The tour was the highlight of the season, giving the *Royal Cornwall Gazette* occasion to print an extended essay, 'Music and Mr. Incledon',[15] in which the development of musical taste was compared to the refinement of the palate for food.

> In early life, the unsophisticated palate is amply gratified with plain and wholesome viands, and the ear delighted with simple melody. But greedy of enjoyment, and cloyed at length by repetition, debilitated Nature seeks support from the crutches of Art. The lax palate of the glutton is stimulated by sauces, till his stomach is surcharged with a chaos of warring elements— the ear of the connoisseur seeks to extract harmony from discord, expand the bravura, or expires on the warblings of an eunuch.

Incledon's appeal, according to the *Gazette* was that it could appeal equally to the simple, honest taste and the sophisticated listener without corrupting the highest standards of taste. In his Truro concerts 'his softer tones dissolved the soul in more than feminine tenderness' but he also displayed 'heroic energy' in his ballad songs. His repertoire in both

Falmouth and Truro represented his most admired operatic roles as well
as popular songs and ballads. In all his performances he gave 'equal
pleasure to the adept in musical science and the lover of simple melody.
His science, indeed, is nature—his nature science'.

Incledon took the opportunity during his visit to Cornwall to return to
his native village

> after an absence of near forty years. The bells were set a ringing on the
> occasion, and every other manifestation of joy and respect was shown by the
> inhabitants to their distinguished parishioner: who, in his turn, treated them
> with princely liberality.[16]

The presence of these visitors, distinguished and less distinguished, did
not distract the gentlemen amateurs from their activities; their only recorded
concert in 1807 received the highest praise in the *Royal Cornwall Gazette* and
'exceeded everything of the kind which has preceded it in Truro'.[17] At this
time however the society was contemplating a more ambitious venture; it
was proposing 'to bring down some of the first rate singers and performers
of the metropolis in the course of the ensuing winter, and to give concerts
on Truro in a stile that shall rival those of the Ashleys'.[18] Like the abortive
festival of 1802 this project did not materialise. It seems probable that it
was impossible to engage sufficient performers to undertake the long and
difficult journey to Cornwall in winter without the financial inducements
of similar festivals in the intervening towns. The music lovers of Cornwall
had to remain content with the scheme for a triennial festival proposed in
1806.

III

The first announcement of the 1809 festival appeared in a brief paragraph
on 23 December 1808, and in February 1809 the management of the Ashleys
was confirmed. Full details of the twelve distinguished stewards, the
performers and outline programmes were published on 22 July 1809. As
in 1806 morning performances of religious music were to be held in the
parish church—a selection of sacred music including Handel's *Dettingen Te
Deum* on Tuesday 5 September, *Judas Maccabeus* on Wednesday, *The
Creation* on Thursday and—inevitably—*Messiah* on Friday. The Tuesday
selection was for the benefit of the Infirmary, as was the Ball which
concluded the festival on Friday evening. On Tuesday, Wednesday and
Thursday evenings concerts were to be held in the Theatre including

'favorite Grand Symphonies, Songs, Solos and Concertos, by the principal performers: and some of the newest and most favorite glees, as sung at the Vocal Concerts.'

The instrumentalists named were largely those who had appeared at the earlier festival, though the name of a local musician, Charles Hempel, organist at St. Mary's, was included as a 'cellist in some of the announcements. Also as before the 'numerous and complete' band and chorus was enlarged 'by the most approved performers, from London, Bath, Bristol, Plymouth and Exeter'. Apart from Goss, the male 'alto, and Vaughan, the tenor who returned 'at the request of our principal amateurs', all the singers were new; their professional status and reputations lacked the drawing quality of the stars of 1806.

One small innovation in the preliminary advertisements could easily escape notice: 'Books of the words' were advertised to be on sale at the Church and Theatre for 6d. each. Though the custom of issuing the libretti of oratorios, often furnished with stage directions, had been common in Handel's day, John Ashley had extended the practice by the inclusion of historical and biographical information, thus providing the earliest annotated programme notes. It is possible that the books on sale at Truro were early examples of this useful and informative service.

In spite of the *Royal Cornwall Gazette's* attempt to generate enthusiasm by describing the gathering audience as 'a company more brilliant than has been witnessed here since King Charles II took refuge in his faithful Cornwall',[19] it would appear that the festival lacked the atmosphere and excitement of its predecessor. On 9 September, a brief, polite notice enumerated the individual performances which were 'on the whole' excellent, though the new principal soprano, Miss Parke, 'did not erase from our memory the powerful and rich swell of Mrs. Dickons.' The attendances were not as great as in 1806 but 'more select and respectable'; from this telling phrase it would appear that the lower ranks of society who were drawn to *Messiah* in 1806 did not return for the second festival.

As far as one can judge from the lack of enthusiasm evident in the reports, the 1809 festival was the least successful of the three early nineteenth century ventures. The main factor must have been the lack of a singer of sufficient reputation or personality to capture and maintain the interest of the audience. 1806 had two such figures: Griglietti whose charm and personality outweighed her lack of experience, captivating the elderly gallants, and Mrs. Dickons, the leading English singer of her day who drew forth equally chivalrous behaviour from admirers. Lord De Dunstanville, on hearing that she was unwell, 'very handsomely sent his carriage to carry her to and from different oratorios and concerts.'[20]

Indeed, it may have been the lack of success experienced by the second festival which caused the abandonment of the triennial pattern; the third and final festival did not occur until 1813, though its success was assured from its announcement by the presence of the most famous and dynamic singer of her day, Catalani.

Angelica Catalani [1780–1849] had made her operatic debut in Venice at the age of fifteen. Her first season in London, 1809, had been marked by riots at Covent Garden at the raising of prices by the management in an attempt to recoup the expense of her salary. She rapidly established herself as a dominant figure on the English stage and became a great favourite during her frequent London seasons and provincial tours. Richard Edge-cumbe, second Earl of Mount Edgecumbe, whose *Musical reminiscences of an old amateur for fifty years from 1773 to 1823*, published in 1824, describes the tastes and artists of his day, analyses Catalani's art and technique in some details.[21] Her voice had 'a volume and strength' that surprised the listener, coupled with an agility in chromatic passages and a wide compass 'in jumping over two octaves at once'. Her technical brilliance however was not always matched by her judgement:-

> . . . her taste is vicious, her excessive love of ornament spoiling every simple air, . . . she is fond of singing variations on some known simple air, and latterly has pushed this taste to the very height of absurdity by singing, even without words, variations composed for the fiddle.

Mount Edgecumbe was of course describing Catalani ten years after her visit to Cornwall, though from the details available of her concerts in Exeter and Truro it would appear that her style changed little in the intervening years. While display, florid ornamentation and technical brilliance at the expense of style would not necessarily appeal to an experienced connois-seur, there is no doubt that it could be a great attraction to a less sophisticated provincial audience. In spite of her affectations even Mount Edgecumbe acknowledged that she was a compelling performer;

> With all her faults therefore (and no great singer ever had so many) she must be reckoned a very fine performer, and if the natural powers with which she is so highly gifted were guided by sound taste and judgement, she might have been a perfect one.

Moreover Catalani's stage presence was—perhaps surprisingly for a *prima donna*—linked with the reputation of great personal kindness and charm; two incidents in her tour of the West—a concert in Exeter Cathedral and her encouragement of a local composer in Truro—appear to reinforce this reputation.

Though Catalani's name and 'divine airs' had been mentioned in the *Royal Cornwall Gazette* as early as December 1808, she was herself a newcomer to the concert world of the West; several of the principal instrumentalists, however, had appeared in the earlier festivals. The direction of the festival was in the hands of John Loder who had been principal second violin in 1806 and 1809. Like the Ashleys, the Loder family produced several well known musicians who left their mark upon English musical life in the nineteenth century. Local musicians, such as Hempel and Christiana, organist at Falmouth, were also engaged to supplement the visiting professionals.

For the first time detailed programmes for all the concerts were printed in the papers.[22] The scale of the festival was reduced from that of the earlier ventures; no oratorios were held in the church, the performances being confined to three evenings at the Assembly Rooms. Two mixed vocal and instrumental concerts on Tuesday and Thursday framed 'a Grand Selection of Sacred Music', including extracts from *Messiah*, *Samson* and *The Creation*, on Wednesday evening. The omission of a complete performance of *Messiah* in the church caused adverse comment, particularly when the papers reported the success—financial and artistic—of the performance at St. Sidwell's Church, Exeter. Flindell's *Western Luminary*, printed in Exeter, of 7 September, stated the position succinctly.

> We ventured (from no slight knowledge of Cornwall) to suggest previous to the performance at Truro, that the *Messiah*, at the church, should form part of the arrangement; and had that been done after *timely notice* of the intention, we are still confident that very many would have attended, who never enter a theatre. This is a piece which it requires neither musical science nor fiddlestick art to comprehend and feel and which never fails to operate upon the taste and religiousness of all orders.

The 'miscellaneous' concerts included a 'grand symphony' by Haydn, concertos by Pleyel, Loder and Percivall, the 'cellist of the company, and overtures by Romberg and, again, Percivall. The vocal works ranged from songs, glees and ballads by fashionable English composers, Storace, Bishop, Doyle, Shield and Davy, to bravura items for Catalani by Portogallo and Meyer and included Guglielmi's 'Gratias agimus tibi' which the star liked to introduce in her performances of *Messiah*.

Truro was 'all bustle and gaiety'[23] during the week preceding the festival as parties assembled for 'a display of talent never before equalled in the

West of England'; lodgings were full in the face of an unprecedented demand created by 'the fame of the musical Syren Catalini'; patrons were requested to present themselves at the door with a ticket 'on account of the scarcity of change'.

The performers gave 'universal satisfaction'. Catalani 'shone in her accustomed strength', her singing of 'Gratias agimus tibi' deserving especial praise for 'her amazing powers and execution' though one of the supporting singers, Miss Nash—'an interesting young lady from Bath'—was applauded for her performance of Arne's 'beautiful and chaste *Hymn of Eve*' which 'received fresh graces from her execution'. In a similar manner it was the virtuosity of the instrumentalists rather than the quality of the music performed which impressed the commentator. Percivall's 'cello concertos showed 'a depth of science, brilliancy of execution and superiority of tone' but Loder's performance on the violin

> exceed the powers of language to describe. The difficulty of the movements, the rapidity of the shifts, the intricacy of the fingering, and the sweetness of the tone rendered his performance a treat of the most superior kind.

It is difficult to assess what impact these festivals had upon the development of musical life in Cornwall. Certainly they were important social events—a 'display of Beauty, Rank and Fashion' attended in 1813— and they provided some encouragement and inspiration for local amateurs and professionals. This encouragement could occasionally take a more practical form than the mere attendance or participation in the concerts themselves. The *Royal Cornwall Gazette* for 17 September 1813 reports a distinguished first performance for the work of a local composer, probably Charles Hempel:

> We understand that the *Te Deum* which was first introduced into the service of St. Mary's church, the composition of a respectable Gentleman of this town, possessor of considerable musical talent, received the most unqualified eulogiums from Madame Catalani, Messrs. Loder, Percivall, etc. during their late visit to Truro. Madame Catalani complimented the author by singing the whole of the composition with that pathos and energy which are peculiar characteristics of her extraordinary powers, and for which she is so deservedly celebrated. She strongly recommended that it should be published.

Whatever benefits did accrue from these provincial tours however do not seem to have outweighed the problems which surrounded them; perhaps the financial rewards were insufficient to tempt the artists to travel west or to encourage the organisers to undertake the complex administrative problems which surrounded such ventures. Whatever may be the reason it is a fact that the pattern of triennial festivals so enthusiastically proposed in 1806 was soon broken and, after 1813, the project was dropped.

Truro 1816
Royal Institution of Cornwall

5

Truro:
Assemblies, Balls and Concerts

Truro is the place of all general assemblies for the south and west of the shire
... The gentry are also enlivened by a philharmonic society, established in
the latter part of the last century. It consists principally of gentlemen amateurs,
assisted occasionally by professional gentlemen, who perform about thirty
concerts annually
        [Gilbert, C.S: *An Historical Survey of the County of Cornwall*, 1817 i,p.818]

As most of the county gentry had their town residencies in Truro, it was
undoubtedly the one Cornish town capable of providing the fashionable
audiences to support regular concerts and musical evenings. Social prestige
clearly played a part, for to be seen and admired in approved company
could provide a valuable aid in advancement in society.

There we often met Miss Giddy who had a certain naivete extremely
interesting, and whose elegant finger on the pianoforte was one of her most
agreeable recommendations.[1]

Even by contemporary standards, Truro society appears to have been
keenly aware of social standing. 'The people of this town' wrote *The
Universal British Directory* in 1791 'dress and live so elegantly that the *pride*
of Truro is one of the bye words of this county'.
    Visitors to Truro generally found it attractive:

I have seldom seen a neater town than Truro; the best streets wide and airy,
with good houses and well furnished shops, all paved in the modern style,
their names at the corners, and the lamps at convenient distances. Everything
here seems improving, and nothing going to decay.[2]

Not all visitors were impressed: Charles Dibdin, the actor and author, wrote in his *Observations on a Tour* [1801] that the town 'for strangers seems to have all the dullness of a city, with but few of its advantages'.[3] Some older members of Truro society may have shared Dibdin's view; on his return to the town to take up a curacy at Kenwyn in 1809, the Rev. Richard Polwhele compared the present dearth of amusement to the period of his youth twenty or thirty years earlier.

Truro was far from the same. It had lost its humour, its jokes, its hilarity.[4]

These views were not, it would appear, generally shared by the inhabitants. Though there was an inevitable ebb and flow over the years in the success of the varied social entertainments available, the newspaper reports continually remark upon the opportunities offered for pleasurable recreation. In addition to the occasional events—royal birthday celebrations and national festivities such as the Peace Treaty with France—there was a constant round of local organisations to offer diversion; if one fell into decline, such as the unsuccessful theatrical season of 1807, there were always compensations.

Our *Elegants* have other assemblies, in which they are seen and admired by all the fashionable gallants who either reside in, or visit the neighbourhood, . . . they have their concerts and harmonics in summer, with the addition of dancing and card assemblies in winter, and elegant conversation parties throughout the year . . .[5]

In Truro, as in almost every town throughout the country, the Assembly was at the centre of most social events. Few towns did not have an entrepreneurial innkeeper who adapted or rebuilt his premises to provide a large meeting room for the balls and concerts which provided the staple diet of entertainment for the social elite of the neighbourhood, and smaller rooms for the popular card and conversation parties. In the larger and more affluent towns purpose built Assembly Rooms were erected, either by private enterprise or by public subscription, to serve the community. Truro's building, combining Assembly Rooms and Theatre was erected in 1787, the money being raised by Tontine. Each of the twenty eight shares was sold at £55, with Lord Falmouth taking three.[6] The building served as a focus for local activities for eighty years.

Assemblies were organised by committees, often under the management of prominent local dignitaries and, to ensure the 'respectability' of the society, membership was restricted to those who paid an annual subscription. Such control over the membership often encouraged those to participate in the Assembly whose social position or personal beliefs would not allow them to attend more public entertainments.

> The merry part of our neighbours have been not a little diverted today, and the grave astonished, at being told by a *Methodist Preacher* of some *notoriety* that he was present last evening at the Truro Assembly, delighted with the 'mazy dance' and in raptures at the 'attentions of the belles'—Poor man! it is feared 'his wits begin to unsettle'.[7]

It was through the assemblies that the subtle interplay of social standing could be established, respectability and acceptability within the community confirmed—or withheld—and liaisons and relationships—personal and professional—developed. A successful assembly needed to reflect all aspects of polite society, and, especially, should achieve a balance of the sexes. The 'plentiful lack' of young men[8] had been a recurring problem of the Truro Assembly which probably caused serious concern amongst the parents of marriageable daughters, and, no doubt, the young ladies themselves! In spite of paying a lower subscription rate—four shillings, as opposed to five for men[9]—women often outnumbered men by two to one.[10] Fortunately the situation was sometimes remedied by visiting officers stationed temporarily in the area.

> Our assembly was enlivened by the presence of several naval and marine officers, who were received with those polite attentions which the honors of their profession so justly entitle them to; they appeared delighted with the fascinations of a Truro assembly.[11]

It was possibly the low subscription rates as much as the dearth of eligible young men that brought a crisis in the affairs of the Truro assembly in 1809–1810. An advertisement placed in the *Royal Cornwall Gazette* on 28 August 1810 by Thomas Warren called for a meeting of 'the ladies and gentlemen who have severally subscribed to the Truro assembly as well as those who intend to subscribe' as the organisation was in financial disarray, in that the 'expenses exceeded the receipts'. It was not simply a matter of raising subscription levels which was needed, though this was done at the subsequent meeting with a massive rise to fifteen shillings for women and to a guinea for men, but a complete reorganisation of the management.[12] Part of the premises 'now in the occupation of Elizabeth Jennings, widow', were to be re-let on an extended lease to increase the income. There were hopes that the assemblies would be revived 'with great spirit' in the coming

winter season provided that intending members indicated their willingness
to subscribe to support the new pattern of events;

> As the Balls are proposed to be carried on upon quite a new Plan, it is
> necessary to ascertain the Number of Subscribers before the Balls commence.

In spite of the urgency of the situation, the first event of the new season
was bedeviled by the old problem: there was

> a respectable assemblage of company but the dearth of *beaux* is remediless,
> and without *beaux* what are assemblies.[13]

Attendances appear to have improved and the new arrangements proved
satisfactory.

> We are happy to find that the unfavourable weather of last evening did not
> prevent the lovers of the 'mazy dance', from attending the second monthly
> Assembly in this place. The blaze of beauty and fashion which attended it
> equalled any thing which had previously been seen at a Truro Assembly.
> About twenty couple kept up the dance with great spirit when this paper
> went to press.[14]

Unusually the paper found it worthwhile to devote valuable space to a
full list of the participants. The regular balls provided employment for
musicians and dancing masters as well as diversions for the two hundred
dancers who would be present at the most popular events such as the
Easter Sessions Ball, normally organised for the benefit of a professional
musician, and the September 'Scholars Ball' with which the season normally
began.

On occasions the Assembly rooms would provide the venue for a
demonstration of the talents of the pupils of a local dancing teacher, as this
colourful description of an event in Penzance shows.

> We had not room last week to do justice to Miss Williams' ball, at the
> Assembly room in Penzance ... On Thursday evening the assembly room
> was graced by a dancing exhibition of Miss Williams' scholars, which was
> truly elegant and pleasing; the steps, figures, and manoeuvres of these
> graceful young ladies, gave infinite delight to the parents and friends of the
> juvenile dancers, as also to a crowded room of genteel visitors. Minuets, figure
> and fancy dances, cotillions, reels, etc. composed the evening's entertainment
> ... She taught the younger nymphs to come 'tripping light as fairy elves o'er
> silver dew',—whilst the more ripe, appeared clad like immortal goddesses,

and beautiful as they are;—here were goddesses of many descriptions, Latonas and Auroras, Vestas and Minervas, Hebes and Cereses; but in that most elegant, graceful and finished dance the minuet, the young ladies appeared like so many Junos, wrapt in the thin mantle of bright cloud, sailing upon the bosom of the air.[15]

Attendance at an event promoted by the assembly was a guarantee that appropriate standards of decorum could be expected; the more public arena of the theatre held no such certainty. An account of another dancing event at Penzance illustrates something of the difference. During a visit to Plymouth in about 1796 the Irish tenor Michael Kelly, still remembered as one of the artists who took part in the first performance of *The Marriage of Figaro* under the composer's direction, fell into conversation with the manager of the town's theatre, Mr. Jefferson. Jefferson and Kelly were old friends who had performed together at Drury Lane, though Jefferson's career had not been as successful as Kelly's and he had spent a period as manager of a band of strolling players in Cornwall. The fortunes of the company were low and, during a visit to Penzance where they staged their performances in a barn, they were joined by a French dancer, La Croix, who had come to seek his livelihood in England.

> When he arrived at Penzance, he waited upon Mr. Jefferson, offered his services, and said that he had no doubt he should draw crowded houses by the excellence of his performance; for Monsieur La Croix, in his own opinion, was 'Le Dieu de la danse'. He was accordingly enrolled in the company on the usual terms, that is to say, that all should share and share alike. He made his appearance in a fine pas seul; but, unluckily, in one of his most graceful pirouettes, a very important part of his drapery, either from its age or slightness, or from the wonderful exertion of its wearer, became suddenly rent in a most unmendable manner. Shouts of laughter and applause followed, which Monsieur La Croix imagined were given for his jumping; nor was the supposition at all unjustifiable, for the higher he jumped, the more he was applauded. At last some one behind the scenes called him off the stage; and he was so shocked at the mishap which had befallen him, that he could never be induced to appear again.[16]

The contrast with the decorous events at Miss Williams' ball could not be greater.

The dances which Miss Williams' young pupils performed, minuets, cotillions and country dances, were also the most popular features of the balls in the early years of the century. After about 1810 a new fashion pointed to a change in popular taste. The quadrille, with its complicated patterns derived from stylised cavalry movements, spread from France and assembly balls began to be advertised as Quadrille Balls. Stationers sold cards which taught the steps and dancing masters advertised their expertise in teaching the new dance. The 'First Quadrille Assembly' in Truro , under the patronage of Vicountess Falmouth was announced in the *West Briton* on 20 February 1818.

Not all the Assembly events were held indoors; most Cornish assemblies took seasonal advantage of the rivers, country-side or coast to organise summer picnics and excursions. Even though the weather was not good, the 'aquatic excursion' of sixty participants which left Truro in a flotilla of pleasure boats, accompanied by the Royal Cornwall Band, had a pleasurable day in August 1818.[17] Instead of dining in the open air at Roundwood, 'one of the most picturesque places as to situation and scenery on the Truro river', the company enjoyed the food—'every delicacy the season could afford'—fine wine and musical entertainment in a spacious building on the Trelissick estate. The party then adjourned to the home of Colonel Gossett which had been decorated

> with festoons of variegated lamps, interwoven with oaks and evergreens; the *tout ensemble* producing a very brilliant and fascinating effect. The floor was chalked with various devices. Country dances and quadrilles were announced . . . after the supper the dance was resumed, and continued with the greatest spirit and vivacity until Aurora denoted the dawn of day, when the party broke up highly gratified with the polite and affable deportment and attention of Col. and Mrs. Gossett. We need only observe that the utmost hilarity prevailed throughout the day.

Though not formally related to the Assembly, the personalities, and events of the Harmonic Society were very similar, and the two organisations were intimately related. Though Gilbert refers to the Truro Philharmonic Society performing 'about thirty concerts annually' there is no documentary evidence to support this; the only well documented account is the sequence of reports covering the winter season of 1803–1804 which appeared in the *Royal Cornwall Gazette*. The first of the reports of the six concerts, held at three to four week intervals from late November to early April, appeared on 3 December 1803. The performers were commended for achieving a style 'seldom heard in a concert of amateurs only'. Subsequent reports complimented the standard of playing and singing which 'gratified a numerous and fashionable assemblage' and the author claimed that 'Truro . . . could boast an Amateur Concert, rarely achieved at this distance from the Metropolis.'[18]

Concerts were held in the members' houses; the hosts were John Vivian [Pydar Street], James Williams [Princes Street, two concerts], James Nanki- vell [Boscawen Street, two concerts] and Colonel Warren, whose rooms were 'peculiarly adapted to this elegant species of entertainment; the spaciousness of which also afforded the company an opportunity of tripping it 'on the light fantastic toe' till a late hour'.

For the musician the significance of these reports is not the light they throw upon the social order of the day but the glimpse they give—albeit slight—of the music performed. Almost all the concerts contained vocal and instrumental music and it is quite clear that the intermingling of songs and glees with instrumental music was a necessity to engage the interests of those whose tastes did not stretch to the sounds of instruments alone; in its report on the second concert the *Royal Cornwall Gazette* makes this point explicitly:

> Our subscription concerts also are in a very flourishing state; but in the latter, we regret that there is no vocal music to vary the entertainment.

The fashion for mixed concerts of instrumental and vocal music was not, of course, confined to the provinces, nor, indeed was it a feature of English musical life alone. The concerts promoted by such distinguished figures as Mozart and Beethoven in Vienna, and Haydn in Vienna and London invariably included vocal items to complement the instrumental fare.

The composers named in the reports—unfortunately individual works are rarely identified—indicate that the baroque idiom which had exercised such a profound hold over English music in the eighteenth century still had an appeal for early nineteenth-century amateurs. The music of Marcello who had died in 1739 and, above all, of Handel whose compositions were included in all four concerts for which details survive, appears alongside that of the more recent classical masters, Haydn, Mozart and Pleyel. A fashionable—though now forgotten—contemporary Bohemian composer, Adalbert Gyrowetz, is represented by the inclusion of a trio and the manuscript glee introduced in the February concert may well have been the work of a local composer. The taste suggested by the composers identified point to a curious blend of a delight in the latest novelties of contemporary composers coupled with an overwhelming respect for the oratorios of Handel, now over half a century old, a respect which had no doubt been fostered by the massive Handel Commemorative Festivals at Westminster Abbey of the 1780s and 1790s.

Technically the music, both old and new, would not have put extreme demands upon the abilities of accomplished amateur performers. A certain fluency and security of technique would be required but equally important would be a quality of taste and style to match the elegant charm of much of the fashionable music.

These early reports stress that the Truro Philharmonic Society was entirely composed of amateurs, but within a few years the involvement of professional musicians, attested to by Gilbert in 1817, begins. Standards generally appear to have been rising and the increasing involvement of professionals in the regular meetings of the society may be assumed before the more publicised benefit concerts became a regular feature of the season. The distinction between private gatherings and public concerts remained, though the private occasions are rarely reported. The review in the *Royal Cornwall Gazette* on 11 July 1807 remains a rare glimpse of these meetings.

> On Tuesday evening at the Concert Room a musical treat was given to a select party of the lovers of that divine science by the members of our Harmonic Society, which in point of execution exceeded everything of the kind which has preceded it in Truro—Both the vocal and instrumental parts were sustained with a degree of ability and execution very rarely to be met with in amateur concerts and which reflected the highest credit on the talents of the several performers. Among the many beautiful glees we cannot omit particularly noticing one by Cummins 'What is friendship but a name' MS. which received the warmest applause and in which the author has evinced a genius which raises him to no inconsiderable name in the profession.

It was probably at a similar event a year later that an anonymous artist drew a group of musicians performing: the sketch is entitled 'A Musical Club'. The drawing is dated in the lower right-hand corner 'Truro, 8 November 1808', and one must assume that the occasion, otherwise unrecorded, was one of the regular meetings of the Truro amateurs; the scale of the portrayed event would also suggest that it was a private event and not one of the more formal benefit concerts. Eleven musicians are gathered round a long table and their performance is observed by a dignified, portly figure standing on the left. Eight players are seated, two 'cellists, two flautists and four violinists. One, or more, of these violinists may be playing a viola, though, from the scale of the drawing, it is impossible to be sure. The three standing musicians are a horn player and his companion—probably a second horn though his instrument is hidden behind his music stand—and, most significantly, a black violinist. This can only be Joseph Emidy and thus we have the only known portrait of the man.

Though there is little doubt that the artist attempted to capture the likeness of the individual performers and that the portraits would have been recognised by contemporary Truro society, there are few clues now to help in identifying the members of the orchestra or the observer. Nor can the location be identified. It is possible that the scene may be set in one of the larger town houses where the Amateurs sometimes met; in which case, the observer could be the host for the evening. The 1807 report, however, refers to 'the Concert Room', presumably part of the Assembly building, and this may well be scene depicted by the artist.

The placing of the players in an inward-facing circle suggests that the music making was for private enjoyment rather than to entertain an audience and the apparently random positioning of the musicians—the separation of the 'cellists at either end of the ensemble in particular—recalls a chamber music atmosphere rather than the more formal orchestral layout of the early nineteenth century. Emidy's standing position would be entirely appropriate for an orchestral leader—conductors were rarely used for orchestras at the time—though his position at the extreme right would not be the most convenient from which to coordinate the performance. Such an ensemble of strings, brass and wind would be entirely appropriate to perform most of the music which, from the surviving evidence, we know that the Truro Philharmonic Society normally performed.

The most highly publicised events of later seasons were the benefit concerts promoted for those professionals who were most closely associated with the society. Two musicians in particular, Joseph Emidy and Charles Hempel, organist at the parish church, featured in these events. Following his first Truro concert and ball in April 1804 Emidy continued to organise a regular benefit evening for the rest of his life; at first these events appear to have taken place spasmodically. In 1806 a ball, jointly promoted with Richard Brown, was 'pretty well attended'[19] but there is no report on the concert and ball held in June 1808 to indicate success or failure. The musical programme included overtures by Handel and Martini, symphonies by Haydn and Pleyel, and a violin concerto by Emidy himself 'composed purposely for the occasion'.[20] The concert for the King's birthday in 1810, patronised by the commander and officers of the Royal Cornwall Militia 'produced rather a select than a numerous company'. The programme and its performance, however, were admired, and Emidy's contribution as both composer and soloist commended.

> In the musical selection and performances of the evening, the excellence of Emidy in his Concerto and Rondo was equally conspicuous, whether we consider the beauty of the composition, which was his own, or the exquisite skill and taste of his execution.[21]

There is no evidence as to whether this concerto was the same work which had been performed in Falmouth in 1804, the new work of 1808, or a third concerto as, like all his compositions, the music is lost.

In the advertisement of his 1815 concert Emidy promised 'a most numerous and complete Orchestra' at the Assembly Rooms and thanked the nobility and gentry for the 'very liberal' support and patronage experienced 'during a period of fourteen years'; he advised all his patrons that he was now resident in Truro and continued to offer his teaching and instrumental repair service.[22]

The Emidy family's new home at 4, Charles Street was close to the most prestigious road in Truro, Lemon Street, where, no doubt, many of his potential pupils had their residences, and close to the premises where most musical parties were held. The early years of the century had seen the development of the handsome terraces which earned Lemon Street the description of being the 'best Georgian Street west of Bath', though the properties on Charles Street were humbler and largely occupied by tradesmen and women who served the needs of the richer inhabitants of the town's major street.[23]

Following his move to Truro, the benefit concert normally became an annual event. Details of the music performed are even scantier than for the earlier ventures as printed handbills were distributed to supplement the newspaper accounts. Occasionally music reflecting current affairs was introduced; the death in 1817 of Princess Charlotte, fully reported in the preceding weeks, was commemorated by 'an admirable vocal piece, first composed by Bishop'.[24] Frequently vocal music was included to vary the diet of instrumental work and, on the few occasions when specific composers are identified, the choice of music offered indicates that Joseph Emidy and his amateur players were in touch with recent music and less inclined to perform older music than their predecessors of 1803.

> Amongst the pieces of music selected for the occasion, are some of the most celebrated compositions of Hayden [sic], Mozart, Paer, Beethoven and Cherubini. The vocal pieces are taken from Stevens, Meyer, Bishop, Horsley and Webbe. Considerable expectations are formed of the gratification that is likely to be derived from such a collection of instrumental and vocal harmony.[25]

Even new developments in instrumental technology could be reflected in the programmes; in the later years of the eighteenth century attempts had been made to extend the versatility of the trumpet by introducing a system of keys, as in wood wind instruments, to allow the instrument to be used fully chromatically, an impossibility on the natural trumpet then in use. Similar experiments were being made with the bugle. Though the new mechanism did not prove fully successful and brass instruments remained restricted in their melodic usefulness until the introduction of valves, the new keyed instruments did have a brief popularity, allowing Haydn, for example, to write his well known trumpet concerto. In a concert in December 1820, in addition to a Grand Concertante by Schneveler, the inclusion of an item for 'two keyed bugles to be performed by a gentleman amateur and Mr. White, of the Cornwall Militia Band'[26] may be taken as an indication that this new technology had reached Cornwall. It is possible, also that the composer of this piece may have been Joseph Emidy, for in the following year, his concert announcement indicates that he had extended his compositional activities to brass instruments.

> Mr. Rowell, from the Royal Cornwall Band, will play a Concerto on the French Horn, which has been composed expressly for the occasion, by Mr. Emidy.[27]

Concert activities were suspended for a period of two years between 1821 and 1823, possibly due to a similar crisis in management which had affected the Assembly twelve years earlier, for, when a resumption was announced, a news report in both local papers pointed to such problems.

> We are much pleased to learn that the Truro concerts which have for years past afforded gratification to the Subscribers, and which were unfortunately suspended for the last two years, are immediately to be resumed under a new system of management, and which, we understand, is calculated to give general satisfaction. The Season will begin with a public concert for Mr. Hempel, ... which we sincerely hope will meet with that patronage which this now celebrated professor of music so justly merits.[28]

The name of Charles Hempel in this announcement introduces to the story a musician who, together with Emidy, occupied a prominent place in Truro music throughout the period. In many ways his career was complementary to that of the African violinist, for Hempel's principle occupation was as organist of St. Mary's Parish Church; his activities as a church musician will be described in a later chapter. Like Emidy, he was building a local reputation as a composer, largely of church music, though, unlike Emidy, some estimation of his abilities can be made as a substantial part of his published music remains. Hempel appears to have been associated with the Truro Philharmonic Society, for he also promoted an annual benefit concert and ball in the town. Hempel's first concert in Truro occurred in 1804, the year in which he succeeded Bennett as organist, and the same year as Emidy presented his first concert in Truro,[29] but it was not until some years after his decision in 1809 to give up his position as a clerk in the Cornish Bank 'to devote his time solely to the MUSICAL PROFESSION'[30] that the concerts became annual events. In 1815 Hempel printed the most detailed programme which survives for any of his concerts, probably in the hope of attracting a large audience to his new venture. Orchestral works, quartets and chamber music by Mozart and Haydn were balanced by popular vocal items, glees by Webbe and Callcott and a song, 'Thro Groves sequester'd' by Hempel himself who also appeared as soloist in a 'cello concerto by Pleyel. A 'numerous and select' orchestra was promised, and, as usual, the entertainment was to be concluded by a ball.[31] Hempel's concerts of vocal and instrumental music became a regular feature of Truro social scene and were usually held in the late summer or early autumn at the opening of the new season. Few details of the music survive, but the events were generally well attended, except when competing attractions tempted the audience away: the concert on 12 August 1818 was

> as usual, got up in excellent style; but we are sorry to add, that owing to the sailing match at Falmouth, and the numerous aquatic parties of pleasure, which the fine weather induced, the company was far from being numerous.[32]

After this date Hempel's concerts were moved a little later in the year, though this move was not always successful in attracting the fickle audience. In 1824 the concert was

> not as fully attended as from the known abilities of that gentleman, and his general favour with the public, there was reason to expect. The pieces selected and the manner of their execution gave entire satisfaction.[33]

Perhaps fickle is too strong a term to apply to the unpredictable pattern of attendance at musical events; the size of the population of Truro—as in every Cornish town—was an inevitable limitation upon cultural events. Within any small community decisions have always to be made in the face of competing attractions and this fact is inescapable. Whilst a visiting artist, well advertised and offering a novelty appeal not otherwise available, was likely to attract a good audience, the locally based musician had to depend to a major extent upon a loyalty built up over a number of years; it was a quality which was hard to win, difficult to maintain, and frequently stressed in announcements of coming events.

He is an old servant of the public, whom we shall be happy to see thus encouraged.[34]

A third professional musician regularly promoted benefit concerts in Truro during the period when Joseph Emidy and Charles Hempel were most active in the town. Mrs. White, however, is an even more shadowy figure and appears to have had no direct contact with the Philharmonic Society. She may have been the wife of Mr. White 'of the Cornwall Militia Band' who played the keyed bugle in Emidy's 1820 concert. She was a singer by profession and, from references within the reports of her concerts, it is probable that she had experience of working in the London musical scene. Her presence in Cornwall remains a mystery for there is no evidence of her offering singing teaching, and, apart from her annual concert and the occasional engagement else-where, her activities pass unrecorded. The first event with which she was associated was a Truro concert in April 1816. Both Emidy and Hempel had advertised their respective first appearances in the locality with particularly detailed notices; later events were promoted with much briefer advertisements, probably supplemented by locally distributed hand bills. Mrs. White, it would appear, adopted a similar practice. Her 1816 concert promised overtures by Mozart—*Cosi fan tutte*—and Cherubini —*Anacreon*; these were followed by symphonies by Haydn and Romberg, a clarinet concerto and vocal items by Shield, Callcott and Bishop, as well as a bravura item by Antonio Sacchini, performed by Mrs. White. The con-cert was to conclude with a performance of Haydn's 'God preserve the Emperor Francis', the new German national hymn.[35] All her advertise-ments for later concerts stress the prominence given to vocal music, as well as the fact that the concerts were not too lengthy to delay the start of the ensuing ball.

More than usual pains have been taken in order that Mrs. White's concert, at our Assembly Rooms, on Tuesday next, may be more than usually pleasing. A greater number of performers than has been usual upon similar occasions, and a judicious, *yet short*, selection, insure satisfaction to the company, and will afford an early opportunity to the dancers to 'sport the light fantastic toe'. From the long and painful, and expensive illness of Mrs. White, we strongly recommend her to the notice of the generous public whom she has so often gratified with her dulcet strains.[36]

Mrs. White's occasional appearances at concerts in other towns usually earned high praise; at the 'second subscription' concert of the season at

Lostwithiel in 1817, the performance of a clarinet concerto by Mr. Arthur was 'deservedly admired'

> but the great attraction of the evening was Mrs. White, who charmed the audience with some of her best songs; amongst which Bishop's celebrated 'Echo Song', was most rapturously applauded.[37]

As with other musicians however, Mrs. White was vulnerable to unpredictable audiences. Though she ensured that vocal items outnumbered instrumental ones so that 'the admirers of the Ball will sooner be engaged in threading the mazes of the airy dance',[38] attendance could often be disappointing. Even the presence of a visiting artist of national reputation was no guarantee that the concert would be profitable. In 1823 her concert was

> but thinly attended. [Mrs. White] though assisted by Mr. Higman from Covent Garden, who with great liberality attended gratuitously, scarcely paid expenses.[39]

'So innocent yet so fascinating an amusement . . .': Concerts across the County

The only personal memoirs which illuminate the Philharmonic Societies and amateur music making, apart from the brief passages in James Silk Buckingham's autobiography, occur in William Tuck's *Reminiscences of Cornwall*, and concern a group of players whose activities are not recorded elsewhere. Tuck had a genuine love of music in all its forms; he presents delightful glimpses of church music in Camborne, appearing to regret the disappearance of the church bands in the face of the new taste for installing organs; writing in the middle of the century, he also enjoyed the increased popularity of military bands, the rise of which he attributed to the volunteer movement. His chief pleasure, however, was music making with friends, a pastime which, in his youth, brought him into contact with Joseph Emidy.

> This predilection [for music] was evinced at Camborne in my early youth, when a few gentlemen combined to meet for musical study and recreation once a fortnight, and engaged a professional from Truro as teacher. This preceptor was a Mr. Emidy, an African negro, who was stolen from his country by the officer of a frigate then on the African coast—they having engaged this genius to play for them at a ball they were holding on board.[1]

Tuck then continues to describe in a passage already quoted how Emidy was plied with drink, awaking to find the ship at sea in passage for England. Emidy was 'the most finished musician' whom Tuck had ever heard and a player blessed with extremely long, thin fingers, not much larger than a goose quill, who out performed any of the other 'stars who have appeared on the London stage during the past fifty years'. The memories of these

Original design for the facade of the Assembly Rooms and Theatre, Truro
Royal Institution of Cornwall

musical evenings of his youth echoed in Tuck's mind many years later when he came to set down his experiences.

> This little party used to assemble at my father's house, when I was permitted to sit in the room, and the pleasure it then afforded me will never be erased from my memory. I well remember two French Horns were used on occasions, and the large number of highly polished rings on these instruments had a great charm for me, although the music produced by them I could never appreciate; they now appear to have become obsolete, for I have not seen one for many years past.

The Camborne orchestra did not survive for long as members died or moved away. Though the survivors attempted to continue to meet and even reformed the society at a later date, fashion had changed and the momentum was lost.

> I believe this happy little band have all been called to the home of their forefathers long since; the last of them was a Mr. J. Rule, of Park Bracket, Camborne, and he would often invite me to spend evenings with him to play duets on our violins. Another valued friendship was that of Mr. Winn, solicitor, who resided at Fore Street, and many a pleasant evening have I spent with him and Mrs. Winn, he playing the hautboy, Mrs. Winn the harp, and I either the violin or 'cello. He was the last of my private musical connections. Sometime afterwards, however, we started a Philharmonic Society, which after some years of successful training, fell into abeyance, from members leaving home or natural sickness and decay, the fate of most such institutions.

Concerts and harmonic societies make occasional appearances in the activities of several Cornish towns, particularly in the 1820s. How far these spasmodic events are a genuine reflection of the true situation, or how much they are the result of limited news reporting, it is impossible to determine. Only two papers served the region, both centred upon Truro, and the affairs of distant towns were not systematically recorded. More probably went on than the surviving records show, but it is almost certainly true that public music making was not a regular feature of any community. Where there is evidence of it developing with any regularity, it is almost invariably associated with the activities of a single individual—generally the organist at the parish church—who provided a focus for the neighbour-hood. The appointment of J.L.Lutman as organist at Bodmin in 1821, for example, saw the development of music making on a new scale in the area. On 11 November 1821 the *West Briton* announced:

An amateur concert has been established at Bodmin, which from the talents
of the performers, bids fair to equal any in the county.

Hitherto there had been few references to music making in the region,
though in 1819 a charity concert at Wadebridge for the benefit of the Scilly
Islanders had drawn upon amateur players from the neighbourhood.

Many Gentlemen amateurs, from Wadebridge, Bodmin, &, &, performed in
the concert, which was allowed by the best judges to be excellent. The
promoters of this most laudable measure have set an example which, we
hope, will be followed throughout the county.[2]

The arrival of John Lutman as organist in Bodmin heralded a significant
growth in music making. Local amateurs provided the musicians for the
first concert early in 1822,[3] but Lutman was soon drawing upon professional talent from throughout the region to increase the variety of music
which his concerts could offer. A lady vocalist from Exeter and Mr. Sharp,
the Falmouth organist, appeared at his next public concert at the end of
the same year,[4] and for the summer concert of 1823, Joseph Emidy and Mr.
Arthur, leader of the Cornwall Band, were the principal attractions.[5] The
young Charles Frederick Hempel, son of the Truro organist and a popular
boy soprano, was engaged in 1826.[6] It is clear that Lutman was very active
in bringing the best of regional talent to Bodmin to give a stimulus to the
work undertaken by his amateur players.

In Helston also musical activity grew in the 1820s following the
appointment of Roger Faning to the post of organist in 1816. Concerts had
been an occasional feature of the town's life in the preceding decade:

On the following night [27 September 1810], the Assembly was crowded with
youth and fashion; a number of gentlemen from the neighbouring towns
were attracted by the display of beauty for which Helston is distinguished.
A concert and Ball succeeded on the following day, and gave such universal
satisfaction as to promise a repetition of a recreation so fashionable and
elegant.[7]

The assembly season and the Flora Day celebrations were usually marked
with balls, and the town's lively social life often had a musical contribution.
In 1811 we find Joseph Emidy's name associated with Helston music, as it
was to be frequently over the next few years.

Seldom have we seen [the Helston School Meeting] more fully and respectably
attended ... Several glees and songs occasionally gave a zest to the

entertainment . . . The dancing [at the ensuing ball] was kept up with great spirit, till the dawn of morning warned the fair votaries of Terpsichore, reluctantly to retire to their pillows . . . [on the following day] between the sets, the company were highly gratified with some selections of music from the best masters which reflected great credit on the powers of the performers and the judgement of Mr. Emidy.[8]

Roger Faning's 'first concert' at the Assembly Rooms was advertised for January 1822[9] when he was assisted by 'a numerous and respectable Orchestra from Truro, Penzance, and other places' and Joseph Emidy's association with the town continued for many years. The *Royal Cornwall Gazette* announced the formation of a Philharmonic Society in Helston in the same issue as it announced the revival of the Falmouth society.[10] The first concert and ball took place in the following December; the orchestra 'which was formed under the superintendence of Mr. Emidy, was so composed as to give universal satisfaction'[11] and the whole occasion was

well and fashionably attended. There was a very full orchestra at the concert, and the whole went with considerable eclat.[12]

As at Bodmin, visiting artists enlivened the concert season; young Hempel planned concerts in Helston and Penzance in July 1825 before his departure from the county to try his fortunes on the national scene, and, as in other towns a visiting novelty could attract a large and curious audience.

On the evening of Wednesday last, Mr. Jacobwitch and his pupil displayed their outstanding vocal powers to a select audience in the Assembly rooms at Helston. The exhibition is, perhaps, of too novel and extraordinary a character to please every ear; but to the lovers of scientific music it cannot fail of affording a very high degree of gratification. The compass and management of the two voices are truly marvellous; and the skill with which they imitate the various instruments, executing the most difficult modulations with the voice alone, is altogether unprecedented in this country. The testimonials which Mr. J. brings with him, from the most distinguished musical professors in different parts of Europe, testify the high esteem in which he has been held by *connoisseurs* and not withstanding certain unfavourable reports by which he was preceded in this town, his hearers felt obliged to him for an evenings entertainment which they will not speedily forget.[13]

Lostwithiel was, like Helston, a town from which the picture emerges of a lively social scene in which music made a significant contribution. Assembly balls, fancy dress and quadrille parties as well an annual regatta were features of the community's life. 'The assemblies of this delightful little town', observed the *Royal Cornwall Gazette* on 21 March 1807, 'have certainly to boast the most full and regular attendance of any in the County'. As with other towns, militia bands were prominent on many occasions, and were very popular at the river regattas. In 1824, thirty-six pleasure boats and yatchs 'mostly decorated with awnings and fancy colours of various devices'[14] sailed from Lostwithiel to Fowey, being joined by more boats for the return trip; welcomed by 'ringing of bells', the party adjourned to the Assembly Rooms.

> ... the weather proved particularly favourable; and, amidst the rich and beautiful scenery of the river, a most numerous and highly respectable company, led on in their little barges by the delightful music of the Cornwall Band; a ball in the evening, resplendent to beauty, added to the attentions and solicitude of the stewards, to meet the wishes of the party, afforded us 'One and All' a day full of pleasure and happy recollections.

As early as 1809 there is evidence of a 'Grand Concert and Ball' costing three shillings and six pence, 'Tea and cards included',[15] but no further details survive for this event. The music lovers of the area also established a subscription concert series at the Assembly Rooms, and, though only occasionally reported, it would seem that, like Helston and Bodmin, an attempt was made to cater for all tastes by inviting prominent musicians from throughout the county to participate; the first subscription concert at the new assembly room was

> numerously attended ... [and] conducted under the direction of Colonel Hext of Restormal Castle, whose performance on the German Horn was deservedly applauded. Mr. White [on] the Key Bugle was much admired, as was the performance of Mr. Emidy on the violin and [?Mr.] Taunton on the Double Bass.[16]

A second concert was held less than two weeks later which

> both in number of auditors, and in variety of performance far exceeded that of the 27th. ultimo. Mr. Arthur's Clarionet Concerto was deservedly admired.[17]

The star attraction, however, was the singing, already reported, of Mrs. White, and especially her performance of Bishop's 'Echo Song'.

This taste of music has inspired the gentry of Lostwithiel, and its neighbourhood, with a general desire, that they may be often gratified with so innocent,
yet so fascinating an amusement.[18]

In spite of the hopes of further musical entertainment of this sort, there
is no evidence that these expectations were fulfilled; concerts do not seem
to have become a regular feature of the town's life, and it may be that the
lack of a professional musician in the area to serve as catalyst for such
events hindered the development. It is quite clear that it was in those towns
where there was both an active social scene and a professional musician—
an instrumentalist like Emidy, or, more frequently, an organist, like Hempel
in Truro, Lutman in Bodmin, Sharp in Falmouth or Faning in Helston—that
regular concerts were most likely to develop. This is not surprising as any
musical society needs a figure who can gather the musicians and music
together, organise rehearsals, extend professional contacts, assemble a
programme and arrange or even compose music to match the local
resources.

It is important also to stress a pattern which emerges from all the
Philharmonic Societies which were active: the concerts were invariably
centred upon instrumental music, using the resources of amateur and
professional players, or local militia bands. Unlike similar occasions later
in the century, or in the twentieth century, there were never choral concerts.
In spite of the popularity and importance of vocal music in church and
chapel, amateur choral societies, whether of male, female or mixed voices,
did not exist. The first evidence of such music-making in Cornwall emerges
in the 1820s in only one town, St. Austell; this is described in Chapter Eight.
Though vocal numbers were often included in Philharmonic concerts, they
were invariably solo items or glees and usually performed by professional
artists resident in, or visiting the area. The few references which occur
describing vocal music being performed by amateurs outside the church
are either in a domestic or convivial setting. Descriptions of society dinners,
Masonic events, or election celebrations often include a passing reference
to the performance of glees—the popular eighteenth-century form for male
voice ensembles—but these are not formal concerts. No doubt such
music-making frequently took place in sociable gatherings reflecting a
continuing tradition of a pleasurable pastime which stretched back through
the eighteenth- and seventeenth-century—there are many references in
Samuel Pepys' diary to such sociable activities—to the popularity of the
madrigal in Elizabethan England which was always a domestic, not a public
affair.

Similarly there must have been many small gatherings of amateur instrumentalists who met to perform chamber music for their own pleasure and who never aspired to give public performances. William Tuck's memoirs give a brief glimpse into such a group in Camborne. The large and varied collection of music assembled by Miss Tryphena Trist which is preserved in the Cornwall County Record Office, gives another remarkable insight into the range of music which was available to the interested amateur. Tryphena of Bowden in Devon married R.M.W. Pendarves, the Cornish MP., in 1804, and brought to her new home a collection of music which no doubt formed the basis of many musical evenings in the following years. The collection consists principally of orchestral and chamber music by composers popular in the early years of the century. Both familiar and forgotten names occur in this collection, the majority of which could be performed by a piano trio—keyboard, violin and 'cello. An arrangement for this combination of the twelve London symphonies of Haydn, together with four volumes of sonatas by the same composer, is the best known music in the collection, but there are collections of sonatas by Dussek, Clementi and Cramer which are still played today. Judging by the amount of his works in her collection, the elegant and graceful music of Pleyel was probably the favourite of Tryphena who possessed no less than thirteen volumes of his music, containing more than forty individual works for piano and strings. Other instrumental composers, now largely forgotten— Mazzinghi, Steibelt, Kalkbrenner and Kozeluch—are well represented, but there is surprisingly little Mozart and no Beethoven, which may indicate that the collection was assembled in the early years of the century before Beethoven's reputation was established. As with any collection of instrumental music, there are missing parts from some of the sets, no doubt reflecting the occasions when individual players borrowed parts to practice before the next meeting, never to return them. The most notable omission is the solo part of a concerto by the now forgotten English composer Griffin, for which a full set of orchestral parts are preserved. The collection included a few song books and popular ballads, two instruction books for the 'cello and part of a manuscript book of piano lessons. There is no way of knowing whether this collection is unusually large or entirely typical of its period; the possession of the music does suggest that Miss Trist had sufficient wealth to indulge her passion for music, so, in this respect, such a wide range of music might not have been available to less affluent music lovers. Nevertheless the collection, assembled as it must have been over a relatively short period and preserved almost intact, may be regarded as a rare opportunity to observe, frozen in time, a glimpse of Georgian taste.

Before we leave this picture of concerts and the intermingling of amateur and professional music making, a final point needs to be stressed. Just as the concert life probably represents only the tip of the iceberg of music making, so the surviving evidence can only represent a fraction of the concert activity. We are dependent upon records which are scanty and not representative of a broad geographical picture. There is no surviving record of concert-giving in Penzance, for example, nor in the towns of north Cornwall. It is very likely that some of the same patterns existed there as in other Cornish towns. Though both Falmouth in the early years of the century and Truro throughout the period were the most active centres, it is impossible to believe that other areas, passed over and largely unreported in the newspapers, had no activity whatsoever. These silent communities remain to be explored.

PART THREE

Church and Chapel

'A strain so grand and impressive': The Church and its Music

Music is perhaps the most vulnerable of the arts. A painting is treasured and preserved on the wall. A book is normally read and handled with care in tranquil surroundings. Musical scores and parts, being the resources for live performances, are marked to give reminders to the players, frequently handled roughly in the tension of performance and individual copies widely dispersed—and often lost or not returned—for practice. When a picture loses is current appeal it may be placed in a cupboard and forgotten; a book takes a unnoticed place upon a shelf. Though age and damp do affect them, they rarely suffer as much as music which has outlived its usefulness. Paintings can be restored and other copies of a book traced, but a set of musical parts—damaged and incomplete—is virtually useless and often destroyed. This is especially true of manuscript music by forgotten composers who, at best, achieved only a local reputation. It is particularly true of church music which has always been an expensive commodity to buy in adequate numbers to furnish sufficient parts for a choir; moreover much published church music may not have been appropriate for the pattern of liturgy used in a particular establishment, nor indeed suitable for the local resources of singers and instrumentalists available. Forms of liturgy have also changed with remarkably rapid pace calling for a continual supply of new music from musicians responsible for matching these needs in church or chapel. Much of the old music was useless and its preservation unimportant; the repair and conservation of the out-dated anthems, hymns or psalm settings was rarely a matter of concern. Only in the largest and most important ecclesiastical establishments, the major cathedrals, where tradition and conservatism led to a continuity of tradition do we find anything approaching a complete record—and it is rarely *totally* complete—of the music.

Music of the parish church or chapel is therefore particularly difficult to document yet, as Nicholas Temperley has pointed out in his important pioneering study, the church 'until recently was the only regular, formal musical experience for perhaps half the population of England'.[1] Through participation in the service, by singing hymns and psalms, by hearing the organ, choir or band where such resources existed, more ordinary people were introduced to musical performance than by any other means. Traditional song and dance, informal music-making of all kinds, must have contributed fully to the experience of many, but it can only have been through church and chapel music that any glimpse of a wider musical culture was achieved by those whose education or income did not allow them to participate in other forms of music making. The church moreover provided one of the few opportunities for a musician, particularly in a rural community, to earn part of his livelihood from his art. In the late eighteenth and early nineteenth centuries few musicians in Cornwall could support themselves entirely from their church employment and most maintained other professional activities as schoolmasters, in commerce or as private music teachers to the local gentry.

All aspects of church life in the period were undergoing a major revaluation and reassessment; church music was no exception. The place of music in the service, the resources used, the nature of congregational participation were all under critical scrutiny. The newly independent chapels of the Nonconformists were also evaluating their theology and redefining their services. In most respects many of these changes pass unrecorded except in the minute books and financial accounts of individual institutions. Personal memoirs, brief notices in the local papers and passing references in the diaries of travellers sometimes give glimpses which supplement the formal records, but essentially it is a story which has not yet been fully told, especially as it affected the fabric of a local community.

The picture which Nicholas Temperley has drawn of the changing patterns of church music in urban and rural communities provides a valuable starting point to commence our survey of the Cornish scene. Following the large-scale destruction of organs and disbanding of choirs in the aftermath of the Civil War, the process of restoring music took a full two centuries in the country churches. In 1801 only 6 of the 273 parishes in Dorset possessed organs, and the picture in Cornwall, as we shall see, was not significantly different. Few instruments had survived the destruction of the seventeenth century; others were more recent instruments often installed through the gift of a wealthy local benefactor or following a public subscription. The early nineteenth century saw a major move to increase the building of churches: following the passing of the Church Building Act of 1818 a million pounds of public money was set aside to finance the building of new churches and during the period 1831–1851 over two thousand new parish churches were erected in England, an average of a hundred a year, compared with an average of sixteen new buildings a year during the proceeding thirty years.[2] This burst of activity, together with a similar programme of refurbishment for older churches, had a tremendous impact upon the growth of organ building though, outside the major cities and larger towns, the cost, both in the provision of the instrument itself and the stipend of the organist—even if a suitable performer could be found—proved a burden for many country churches who avoided the issue and tried to find alternative solutions.

Though the possession of an organ and the employment of a suitable performer remained the aspiration of most parochial councils one alternative which many smaller churches adopted was the installation of a barrel organ. Constructed like a pipe organ and including stops to vary the timbre, the barrel organ was operated by a metal barrel with raised pins which activated the flow of air to the appropriate pipes: each barrel had a repertoire of ten to fifteen hymn or psalm tunes and could be interchanged to provide a wider selection of music. It required no musical expertise to operate and, by avoiding the salary of a trained organist, it appeared to many church authorities an ideal way of providing a sound musical foundation for the services at a relatively modest cost. In practice, however, the inflexibility of the instrument and its limited repertoire proved a hindrance rather than an advantage and churches which had adopted the expedient often found themselves raising funds to replace their barrel organ with a manually operated instrument within a few years.

The scarcity of organs however did not mean that musical contributions to the services inevitably lacked instrumental participation. Church bands became increasingly popular after 1770 and their presence was often taken into account by the compilers of psalmody books which provided the main musical material for many services. These ensembles, usually comprising two to six instrumentalists, appear to have originated in Northern England though they continued in the South West until the end of the nineteenth century, long after the practice had declined elsewhere; a survey of the Truro diocese undertaken in 1895 reported eighteen of the 219 parishes 'using orchestral instruments, varying from a fairly complete band down to a single cornet'.[3] The activities of the church musicians form a major element in Thomas Hardy's *Under the Greenwood Tree*, and the presence of amateur instrumentalists within the communities must have had an impact upon the wider life of the town or village. A.L.Rowse gives a delightful picture of music-making within his family in the St. Austell area in the early years of this century. His uncle's family had a home full of instruments—

> Each of them had his own, some of them could play two or three, and together they constituted a little band which entertained and amused the village and led all its frolics. Even my father took part in the music which was the best part of their activities and which reached its high point with Christmas time, New Year and Twelfth Night.[4]

This evidence of instrumental activity is of course much later than the period under consideration; of instrumental participation in early nineteenth-century church services in Cornwall the information is very scanty.

Even where there were no organs or instruments music did play an important part in many church services. There was a strong tradition of unaccompanied vocal music, unconnected with the cathedral style of polyphonic singing, but created in response to amateur need and parish usage. Temperley describes this music as:

> a characteristic style of singing developed entirely spontaneously by oral transmission from generation to generation, without effective interference by church authorities or professional musicians. In the eighteenth century parish choirs arose, at first in response to the wishes of church leaders, but soon they became more or less free of clerical control and developed a musical life of their own.[5]

What Temperley has identified could almost be described as a folk tradition, closely related to the growth of metrical psalm tunes and verses and popular in a wealth of publications throughout the eighteenth century. Foremost among these publications were Tate and Brady's *Metrical Psalms* which passed through more than one hundred and thirty new editions between its first appearance in 1691 and the 1830s. The memorably simple words and melodies provided a framework for a variety of harmonisations and elaborations by local congregations under the leadership of a singer who would announce the tune and set the pitch. This figure—rarely a professionally trained musician—assumed a position of great respect and responsibility within the congregation and, as Rowse again testifies, continued in rural areas long after the tradition had died out elsewhere; it was a particularly important position in the non-conformist chapels.

Mr. Tredinnick, the town missionary, used to come there and preach. And 'pitch the tune'. Pitching the tune was a very important performance and highly thought-of ability. It demanded not only voice but confidence, not merely confidence but judgement: in short, a head. Granny Varison, my mother's mother, could pitch the tune, and sometimes used to pitch it at prayer meetings at chapel. The old people used to set great store upon not giving out the same tune twice in the course of a day. No hymn books: only the preacher had a hymn book and gave out each verse, told them the tune and they would sing after.[6]

This oral, congregational tradition was at the heart of the new forms of worship associated with nonconformity. The Wesleys recognised the powerful effect of memorable words associated with strong melodies to supplement the spoken word and their influence throughout the country, and particularly in Cornwall, had an enormous influence in reinforcing the tradition of a congregationally based musical tradition. It was a style which was to retain a hold into the twentieth century and which certainly played a part in the development of the local traditions of original hymnody and carols which flourished in the mining districts, perhaps best represented in the music of Thomas Merritt.

It is probably too late now to disentangle myth and reality in the history of the carol. The restrictions on Christmas festivities imposed during the Commonwealth era brought an end to the courtly art carol which had been a significant feature of English vocal music during the late medieval and renaissance periods. When the restrictions were lifted after the Restoration of Charles II in 1660, the carol form did not re-emerge in sophisticated circles. The popular traditions of the carol, however, were less affected by these restrictions and, in the perceptive words of the Preface to the *Oxford Book of Carols*, 'travelled underground and were preserved in folk song.' In truth the folk traditions of the carol had always existed alongside the art form and, particularly in rural areas, remained. Such traditions could not be easily submerged by government or religious prohibitions. After the Restoration the popular carols were circulated orally and, like the popular ballads, were printed in broadsheets. It was not however until the early nineteenth century that a scholarly antiquarian interest in preserving and collecting examples of this tradition emerged. Though some attention had been paid to carols in Percy's *Reliques* [1765] and Ritson's *Ancient Songs* [1790], it was the publication of two books in the early 1820s which first drew serious attention to a form which was in a real danger of being lost altogether. Indeed, almost all collectors and writers of the period speak as though the form was already a thing of the past, the remains of

Engraving by Samuel Cousins from the painting of Henry Howard: Davies Gilbert,
President of the Royal Society.
Royal Institution of Cornwall

which were rapidly disappearing. William Hone's *Ancient Mysteries Described; Especially the English Miracle Plays* [1823] stated that the celebration of Christmas in traditional festivities, including the singing of carols, retained its strongest hold in Ireland and Wales; English celebrations were less popular and, in Scotland, the traditions were not observed at all. Davies Gilbert, whose publication of eight traditional carols in *Some Ancient Christmas Carols* predates by a year Hone's book, describes the festive and ecclesiastical use of carols in the West of England.

Gilbert had been born in March 1767, the son of Edward Giddy who held the curacy of St. Erth. His education was largely undertaken by his father and private tutors due to the boy's poor health, though he attended Penzance Grammar School for a short period. In 1785 he entered Pembroke College, Oxford, taking his degree in 1789. His 'principal delight lay in the company of literary men'[7] and his later career was marked by the pursuit of a wide range of scholarly and antiquarian interests, bridging the arts and sciences. He was elected Fellow of the Royal Society in 1791 and developed a specialised knowledge of the geology and mineralogy of Cornwall which was to remain an active interest for the rest of his life. He was instrumental in 'bringing forth into the sunshine of public encouragement the talents of Sir Humphry Davy'[8], and managed to combine his intellectual interests with a busy political life; he was successively Member of Parliament for Helston [1804] and Bodmin [1806], the obituary in *The Gentleman's Magazine* describing him as 'one of the most assiduous that ever sat in the House of Commons . . . [being] very remarkable for the brief periods which he spent in rest'. Following his marriage in 1808 to Mary Anne Gilbert, Davies Giddy became Davies Gilbert following an injunction in the will of his wife's uncle and moved to live in Eastbourne on his wife's estate, though his interest and involvement with the affairs of his native county did not diminish. This interest found expression both in public honours and in literary work, notably the four volume *Parochial History of Cornwall*, published in 1838. Gilbert's work on the history of the carol is a slighter work but still retains significance as one of the pioneer collections of a disappearing tradition. The success of the 1822 collection of eight carols with their traditional melodies was something of a surprise to the author and, as the *Advertisement to the Second Edition* announces, he decided to issue a new and enlarged collection;

> The small collection of Christmas Carols, printed last year, having attracted much more of public attention than the Editor could have flattered himself with their being likely to obtain, and a Second Edition being called for, he has procured several other carols from the same part of England,

including one appropriate to each of the three holidays immediately following Christmas Day; but he has not succeeded in his best endeavours to get more of the ancient Tunes.

Everything in the tone of the collection indicates that Gilbert felt that he was describing a dying tradition; as he writes in the *Preface*;

> The following Carols or Christmas Songs were chanted to the Tunes accompanying them in Churches on Christmas Day, and in private houses on Christmas Eve, throughout the West of England, up to the latter part of the late century.

He was anxious to stress that the apparent deficiencies in the language had been deliberately preserved as they represented a picture of older idioms;

> The Editor is desirous of preserving them in their actual forms, however distorted by false grammar or by obscurities, as specimens of times now passed away, and religious feelings superseded by others of a different cast. He is anxious also to preserve them as an account of the delight they afforded him in his childhood, when the festivities of Christmas Eve were anticipated by many days of preparation, and prolonged through several weeks of repetitions and remembrances.

Gilbert gives a delightful picture of the celebrations of Christmas in his childhood; as with all major festivals, Christmas was prefaced by a period of fast, though

> when austerities cease, and rejoicings of all kinds succeed. Shadows of these customs were, till very lately, preserved in the Protestant West of England. The day of Christmas Eve was passed in an ordinary manner; but at seven or eight o'clock in the evening cakes were drawn hot from the oven; cyder or beer exhilarated the spirits in every house; and the singing of Carols was continued late into the night. On Christmas Day these Carols took the place of Psalms in all the Churches, especially at afternoon service, the whole Congregation joining; and at the end it was usual for the Parish Clerk to declare, in a loud voice, his wishes for a merry Christmas and a happy new year to all the Parishioners.

The 1823 volume includes twenty carols and six other traditional pieces—four vocal pieces and two dances, including 'The Helston Forey Dance'. Gilbert has some interesting observations about this dance, relating it to 'Celtic Musick . . . heard in Ireland and in Wales' at bonfires celebrating the summer solstice.

> In Cornwall it is almost peculiar to the town of Helston, where a Forey was annually celebrated up to recent times, with all the pantomime of a predatory excursion into the country, and a triumphant return of the inhabitants dancing to this air. Some shadow of the festival is even still preserved in the more elegant amusements of the eighth of May, but with its nature totally changed, and its name obscured, by a fanciful allusion to Greek or Roman mythology.

Of the twenty carols, Gilbert could only provide the melodies for the eight carols which had appeared in 1822, together with a new tune, 'Christians, awake! salute the happy morn', which had been communicated to him from Yorkshire following the appearance of the first collection. It would be interesting to know, for example, whether the melody for 'The First Nowell', the words of which appear in the 1823 volume, was the familiar one which we now know or whether Cornwall had a distinctive tune of its own. Nevertheless the eight melodies which Gilbert did collect include a number of melodies, such as 'A virgin most pure', which are still familiar from their inclusion in later collections such as *The Oxford Book of Carols*.

A number of the melodies and texts which Gilbert included in his collections also appeared in William Sandys' *Christmas Carols Ancient and Modern* [1833]. Sandys was equally pessimistic about the ultimate survival of the carol; though the music was still performed 'in the Northern Counties and some of the Midland', the customs appeared 'to get more neglected every year'. It is clear that the individual writers who first turned their attention to the popular carol and played an important part in the survival of traditional tunes and melodies were not attempting a systematic study of the form throughout the whole country; they were preserving the music, very often, of their childhood and the regions of the country with which they were familiar. This should not denigrate the value and importance of their contribution to the survival and preservation of the traditional material; without such individual efforts and enterprise much material would have been lost for ever. Where we must be careful however, is placing too much reliance on their statements that the carols and Christmas festivities only survived in particular regions. It will already have been noticed that Ireland, Wales, the West, North and Midlands have already been identified as regions in which such traditions survived. Most of the British Isles are thus covered. What does link the regions which the early writers named, is that they were predominantly rural regions and, in particular, regions in which the hold of nonconformity was strong.

Though many of the carols collected by Gilbert have West Country and Cornish origins, it is not possible to claim them with any certainty as specifically and uniquely local in origin; it is evident from any study of folk music that popular lyrics and melodies spread widely, often with subtle local variations, but the true origin of the material is lost in antiquity. What the collection shows, as does the regional material in Sandys' publication, is that the festivities which fostered the performance of carols were still alive in the South West, even if their survival was vulnerable.

The existence of the folk carol tradition at the beginning of the nineteenth-century is in itself not sufficient to explain the emergence in later years of the century of a new tradition of carol composition. The roots of the late nineteenth-century carol are probably more distinctly found in the hymn singing of the Nonconformist churches. Whilst the Anglican church in the eighteenth-century fostered psalmody as the chief congregational musical element, the Nonconformists, following the models created by the Wesleys, favoured hymns. The two traditions moved close together in the early nineteenth century. In the middle years of the century a new species of Christmas hymns emerged alongside the older traditional carols, and it is with this movement that the amateur composers who contributed to the Cornish Carol movement can be associated. That story, however, lies beyond the scope of these pages, though its roots can perhaps be traced to the early years of the century.

The love of hymn and psalm singing also moved outside the churches and chapels into the daily life of the communities; many references can be found to spontaneous performance of devotional music whenever people gathered together. This could be in the home, as the memoirs of William Murrish, a local preacher known as the 'Miner of Perranzabuloe', describes;

> We could all sing, and frequently in the evening struck up a tune. James sang bass, Martin the air, my sisters Nancy and Sally first and second treble whilst father and mother, who had both been church singers in their day, would also join in.[9]

As Martin sang the melody line it is quite clear that the Murrish family held to the old way of performing their devotional music where the principal tune was sung by the tenor voice in the middle of the texture, rather than being performed by the highest voice of the ensemble, usually the treble.

Music might also be used for personal consolation, as the obituary in the

West Briton for 20 October 1826, for the eighty-three year old John Jolyan of St. Austell records; the old man had been

> for more than half a century clerk of that parish, and, from the seventh year of his age a constant church singer . . . (following a stroke four years before his death) he appeared cheerful and happy and when alone was generally repeating and singing Psalms.

Psalm and hymn singing held its place in festivities and celebrations of every kind; Wesley himself records the power of massed voices at Gwennap Pit:

> no music is to be heard on earth comparable to the sound of many thousand voices, when they are all harmoniously joined together singing praises to God and the Lamb.[10]

On formal occasions psalm-singing took a natural place. Eight thousand people attended the laying of the foundation stone of the new church at St. Day, according to the *West Briton* for 13 October 1826, and the musical celebrations were provided by an ensemble of singers and instrumentalists 'playing and singing appropriate pieces'; the formalities over, 'some appropriate psalms were then sung'. There is an implication in this report that the spontaneous performance of the psalms was no longer at the centre of the organised celebrations; this feeling is also evident in other contemporary records. Whatever place community psalm singing held in the hearts of the people—and there is no doubt that its hold was strong— there was a clear move on the part of the Church authorities to consider it outmoded, old-fashioned and not in keeping with the new spirit of the nineteenth century; a condescending tone is distinctly apparent in the report given in *The Royal Cornwall Gazette* (26 October 1806) of an event at St. Germans.

> The venerable aisles of the Cathedral Church of St. Germans, echoed on Sunday last to strains of harmony at once solemn and sublime . . . The Choristers of the parish of Stoke attended, amounting to sixty vocal and instrumental performers. They sang several fine anthems in a masterly manner; and were so *unfashionable* as to give the good old 100th psalm (one of the finest pieces of music extant) and a strain so grand and impressive, as thrilled the hearts of every one that heard it.

It is quite apparent that the Anglican Church in Cornwall was following the trends described by Temperley throughout the country in trying to reform its liturgical practice by exercising more control over its musical content by introducing a more professional content to its organisation. One aspect of the movement was the growing desire to introduce organs. As Dr. Busby wrote in 1820

> an instrument powerful enough to drown the voices of the parish clerk, charity children, and congregation, is an inestimable blessing.[11]

Not all clergy shared this view however. The Rev. E.Shuttleworth wrote of St. Mary's, Penzance in the 1840s that 'the whole service [is] intoned admirably without instrumental accompaniment'; the presence of an organ destroyed the true principle of church music 'burdening the parish in many cases with a stipend equal to, or greater than, that of the curate'[12]. The Rev. Coleridge, newly installed vicar of Kenwyn near Truro, had high ideals of reform when one of the first acts of his incumbency was to set up a subscription to install an organ in the church. There was certainly opposition to the proposal; when considering

> the best method of improving the singing in Kenwyn Church, which of late has been dependent upon the exertions of a single individual, having for some time been in agitation; it appeared to the Rev. Mr. Coleridge that a hand organ would be the most effectual and certain method of leading the congregation in that part of the divine service.[13]

His argument was that the instrument—presumably a barrel organ—would be a considerable financial saving of the current expense of £11–£12 per annum, and after considerable opposition from some parishioners 'especially in a quarter from whence it was least expected', the proposal was carried though the full cost of £90–£100 must be raised by subscription as the parish agreed to pay annually £20 'to get rid of the perpetual tax for singing'. Rev. Coleridge further challenged the conservatism of his parishioners when, less that three months later, he proposed moving the pulpit from the North to the South aisle 'to avoid draughts'.

These were not isolated battles but part of a transformation in church music which had implications beyond the individual parishes. Those churches which possessed or installed organs, for whatever reason, required organists to play the instrument; many churches and chapels who could not afford the instrument and organist nevertheless wished to develop trained choirs to replace the traditions of congregationally based singing; this implied a trained—and paid—choir leader, generally known as a 'singing master'. Though it took the best part of century to complete this transformation a fundamental change was affecting church music from the early part of the century; however much congregations wished to retain the older oral tradition, the organised church choir increasingly became an established fact. Not only were standards of musical literacy beginning to rise as increasingly choristers were expected to read music, but the musician in charge—organist or singing master—was expected to provide, arrange or compose appropriate music for those in his charge. This new movement affected both the Anglican parish church and the nonconformist chapel.

This tendency towards the choir as opposed to the congregation had already become noticeable in some of the newspaper reports already mentioned; it was the *choristers* of Stoke who performed at St. Germans in 1806 and the *singers* who provided musical items at the laying of the stone at St. Day in 1826. Many references to choirs performing specialised music can be found in contemporary records;

> The Weslyan Methodists of Launceston also celebrated [Coronation Day] in a manner suitable to the known feelings of this respectable sect. At an early hour, the choir which attends their chapel, gratified the inhabitants by singing, in different parts of the town, the celebrated Coronation Anthem by Martin.[14]

William Tuck in his *Reminiscences of Cornwall* recalls his life in Camborne in the early years of the nineteenth century; through talking to older friends his account stretches back into the preceding century, and even if his dating of events may be questioned, his amusing stories of church choirs and the problems associated with the barrel organ merit preservation;

> I am well informed that during the latter part of the seventeenth century the musical part of the Church Service was sung by men who used to *wear* leather breeches and buff gloves, standing in front of the orchestra, and each beating time by giving a slap on his pantaloons thus emphasizing the tonic in the scale. The instruments used on this occasion were Bassoons, Bass Viols, Flutes, Fiddles, Clarionets, etc. I remember, and just as far back as my memory serves me, hearing a very old gentleman, Capt. Simon Vivian, who had been one of the choir, speak of this performance of sacred music in a very amusing way. About this time it became disorganised, the common fate of such choirs. The service at this time was indifferently performed and unreliable, so much so indeed that it was decided to have an organ, but here another difficulty arose as to how the funds could be obtained to pay the salary of an organist. Finding that contributions fell short of the necessary sum, it was decided to have a barrel organ which was supplied with a copious index of Psalm tunes, but even with that aid the most ridiculous mistakes would sometimes occur.

The clerk who was the precentor, would give out the wrong psalm for the music set for that day's service or *vice versa*. This caused such confusion that the incumbent and congregation decided to consult the maker as to the feasibility of altering the said instrument into a manual, which was soon done. The control of the musical part of the service was then conducted by two members of the clerk's family in addition to himself; so here under the dome of St.Martin everything now went on as harmoniously as a peal of marriage bells, or indeed until they were stilled by the hand of time.[15]

Some of the more ambitious choirmasters began to take their choirs out of the context of the services and to present concerts. Though this practice had occurred for special events such as the Launceston celebrations of the Coronation of George IV the idea of concert-giving was a new direction which was to have a major impact upon the pattern of musical life away from the county's larger centres. In Cornwall the first evidence of choral concerts appears to be associated with the activities of the St. Austell Parish Church choir under the direction of their singing master Bennett Swaffield in the early 1820s.

Bennett Swaffield and the St. Austell Choir

In the late eighteenth and early nineteenth centuries many visitors to St. Austell commented favourably on the imposing nature of the Parish Church in what most observers considered an otherwise unremarkable town. In 1797 the young Rev. John Skinner recorded in his diary[1] the growing population of the town following developments in tin mining and processing, though commenting that 'the streets are very narrow, and not having any pavement for foot passengers are somewhat unsafe.' The importance of the town had increased after 1760 when the turnpike road from Plymouth to Falmouth had been diverted to pass through it, and with the industrial expansion of the early nineteenth century. Its population grew significantly from the 3686 of the census returns of 1811 to 6175 in 1821. The atmosphere of the town was probably very similar to that described by Murray in 1859 in his *Handbook for Travellers in Devon and Cornwall.*

> It is seated on a southern slope of one of the great hills, and is a place of some bustle from the continual transit through its streets of heavy waggon-loads of china clay for the harbours of Par and Charlestown. It is an old-fashioned and somewhat gloomy town, but can yet boast its cheerful villas on the outskirts.

The 'handsome fabric' of the church—particularly the fifteenth century additions, with the 'fancifully ornamented' tower caught Skinner's imagination as they did those of most visitors:

> various carvings, monstrous heads, angels, and other figures appear on the cornices. Round the second story of the Tower, are eighteen statues in rich ornamented niches: six on the West side, and four on each of the others . . . The shields or ornaments on the outside of this fabric, are also carved on many of the seats; and from the repetition of the shovel, pick axe, and

St Austell Parish Church, 1822

hammers, and other tools, it seems probable that the Miners were the principal contributors towards the expenses of the building.

No visitor, however, remarks upon the presence of an organ within this imposing building. Along with a number of other churches in the 1820s the parish church of St. Austell was considering ways of improving the musical contribution to its services. Like many other establishments a decision to install a barrel organ appeared the best compromise between financial and musical considerations; the sum of £150 was set aside to purchase one.[2] Later a two-manual instrument was installed to replace it; though Canon Hammond, the historian of the parish, does not date the arrival of the new instrument, it was probably during the Victorian refurbishment of the church that this took place. What musical standards the church had possessed before the 1820s is difficult to determine though there is evidence of a continued tradition of choral singing; the obituary of the 83 year old John Jolyon, printed in the *West Briton* of 20 October 1826 describes the deceased as

> for more than half a century clerk of that parish, and from the seventh year of his age a constant church singer.

Hammond notes that in 1814 twenty pounds annually had been voted from the parish rates for the singing 'which is of late very much improved', so we may assume that the church paid serious attention towards the promotion of a good standard of music.

During the 1820s the activities of the parish church choir, under the direction of Bennett Swaffield, became a feature of the accounts of musical events noticed by the newspapers. No record of instrumental concerts taking place in the town has been found, but the performances of the choir, both in contributing to the services and, more significantly, in giving concerts of sacred music, are the first real evidence anywhere in Cornwall of the beginnings of the amateur choral tradition which was to grow in importance as the century progressed.

Unlike musicians at Bodmin, Falmouth and Truro, Swaffield was never called 'organist' in these reports but invariably described as 'Teacher of the Choir'; the modern designation would be choirmaster. This supports the view that, at the period of his appointment, the church did not possess a full organ. The *Bibliotheca Cornubiensis* provides most of the known biographical details. He had been born in Beaminster, Dorset, in March 1796, but the date of his move to St. Austell, or the reasons for it are not known. It is probable that he came as young man in his early twenties to further his musical career by filling a vacancy for a choirmaster at St. Austell, but no advertisement for the post has yet been discovered. Few provincial organists or choirmasters could manage financially on the church salaries and Swaffield supplemented his income from music with a clerical post in the St. Austell solicitors firm of Messrs. Coode. In the 1830 edition of Pigot's *National Commercial Directory* he is identified as 'Inspector of Corn Returns' for the St. Austell district. In 1827 he married Helena Walker and remained in the town until his sudden death in October 1854. The identically worded death notices in the *West Briton* and *Royal Cornwall Gazette* give his age as 55, though according to Boase and Courtney he would have been 58. In the *Bibliotheca Cornubiensis* he is described as 'organist' so it is probable that the replacement of the barrel organ by a full instrument took place during the thirty or more years when he was responsible for musical activities in the church.

There is no doubt that it was due to Swaffield's enthusiasm that the innovations in concert giving in the 1820s took place, matched, presumably, by a good standard of music for the liturgy. The concerts normally took place at the parish church and normally included a selection of anthems, psalms and solos; occasionally there was a modest instrumental accompaniment introduced to support the choir.

> . . . a miscellaneous selection of Sacred Music was performed, by the choir to a numerous and most respectable audience. The progress the choir has made is highly creditable to the talents and taste of Mr. Swaffield the teacher. The recitative 'Like as the dew of Hermon' in Hooper's anthem from the 133rd Psalm, was given with great effect by Miss Nancollas, as were several solas [sic] from other anthems. In Kent's anthems, from the 37th chap. of Job, 'Hearken unto this, O man' and the 29th. Psalm, 'Give the Lord the honor due', the solas were sung with unusually good taste, by Miss Nancollas and Mr. Tremelling. The choir were greatly assisted by Mr. Roscola's violoncello.[3]

Inevitably the music of Handel appears in a number of concert reports, and in 1826 the choir performed 'for the Benefit of the Distressed Manufacturers in Lancashire' in a concert which raised a collection of £20-0-6 for the cause and which gained further praise from the correspondent of the *West Briton*.

> Independently of the pleasure the audience felt in the object of the performance, they were highly gratified by the manner in which the various pieces from Handel, Kent and others, were sung, and which reflects the greatest credit on Mr. Swaffield, the Teacher of the Choir, to whom additional

praise must be given of assisting so excellent a cause by the exercise of their abilities.[4]

Swaffield and his choir did not confine their performances to the parish church but gave some of their concerts in other suitable premises. In the same year as their charity concert they made a small contribution to the ecumenical movement!

> On Sunday evening last, the body of singers which compose the Church Choir, attended Divine Service at the Independent Chapel, St. Austell: at the conclusion of which some pieces were sung with good effect under the direction of Mr. Swaffield. The Chapel was much crowded.[5]

Like many provincial musicians Swaffield composed and some of his work survives. The *West Briton* advertised on 1 March 1822 the publication of a volume called *Sacred Harmony* 'for the use of Churches and Families'.[6] The announcement promised twenty five original melodies for new versions of the Psalms and two anthems and the author was appealing for a subscription list to finance publication; the music was to be published by Falkner's Opera-Music Warehouse of Old Bond Street, London and sold at a cost of seven shillings and six pence through booksellers in the principal Cornish towns. The advertisement was repeated in the *West Briton* on 4 October 1822, possibly after Swaffield had put together his list of subscribers, though, in an advertisement a month later for the sale of a 'very fine toned CREMONA violin' for eight guineas[7] there may be a sign that he had to realise personal assets to finance the printing of his music.

Twenty Five Original Melodies—the published collection has a more prosaic title than the advertised *Sacred Harmony*—consists of psalm settings, two sanctuses, a dismission, a group of wordless psalm chants and a short anthem. All the psalm settings are drawn from Tate and Brady's *A New Version of the Psalms of David* which was a popular source of words for hymnody and devotional music throughout the eighteenth century. The fact that Swaffield was using these poems more than a century after their first publication is an indication of the long-lived success of Tate and Brady's achievement. In their own way 'Tate and Brady' had become as much a part of the common fabric of devotional language as the Authorised Version of the Bible or Bunyan's *Pilgrim's Progress*.

The spirit of eighteenth century hymnody also pervades the music; all the pieces are written for four part chorus with occasional passages for solo voices, together with a simple accompaniment playable either on the piano or organ without pedals. One can be quite certain from the layout of the music that the choral alto parts were written for men's, not women's, voices. There is no way of determining whether the highest part was for male or female voices. Swaffield certainly used a woman soloist—Miss Nancollas— in his concerts, but the dominant Anglican tradition was for boys to sing the highest part in church music; one suspects that a similar tradition was followed in St. Austell. The texture of the music is predominantly homophonic with few contrapuntal passages to tax an average choir or domestic singers. The harmonic idiom is straight-forward as the music has none of that cloying chromaticism which was to taint so much devotional music in the Victorian era. There are graceful, flowing melodies in 3/2 time characteristic of many fine eighteenth century hymn tunes in nine of the items, and many of the remainder in variants of common time have a hymn like character. A few pieces—'To God, the mighty God', 'Praise ye the Lord and 'Just judge of Heav'n'—are on a more ambitious scale, contrasting music in different metres and use a more varied blend of solo and chorus passages. Though Swaffield's technique as a composer shows some limitations, especially in his command of harmony and in the generally unambitious accompaniments, at his best in a vigorous setting like 'Jehovah reigns' or in the touching simplicity of 'Have mercy Lord', there is a direct dignity unmarred by technical weakness.

Bennett Swaffield is not a lost genius; his music does not merit revival except out of a sense of curiosity, yet it does illuminate some details of church music for which there is little other surviving evidence. It is also particularly fortuitous that the music of one of the pioneers of choral music in the region has survived.

'None but persons of ability and good moral conduct need apply': Organs and Organists

There is no complete record of the parish churches or chapels which possessed organs at the beginning of the nineteenth century but such publications as C.S.Gilbert's *An Historical Survey of the County of Cornwall*, published in two volumes in 1817 and 1820 and *The Universal British Directory* of 1791 give us some indication of the existing situation. Some parishes which formerly had instruments had never replaced them after the destruction of the Civil War; Veryan and St.Ives are two examples of this situation. Of the latter, Gilbert wrote

> it had formerly a screen, or rood loft, over which was an organ, that cost £300, and may be supposed to have been the first that was ever put up in Cornwall. It was taken down by order of the sect that composed the parliament in 1647. Mr. Hicks saw many of the pipes, and says they were of a large size.[1]

The parish churches of Callington ('a small organ at the west end'), Launceston ('a fine old organ'), Crowan, Penzance—both possessing 'neat' instruments—Camborne, Bodmin, Helston ('a fine organ'), Falmouth ('a good organ') and Truro were all recorded as possessing instruments by Gilbert. Other towns and churches, though described, are not identified as owning instruments and this may be regarded as a reasonably accurate picture of the situation in 1820.

The information can be supplemented on occasions from other records; we get glimpses of the personalities who filled the position of organist, passing references to their involvement in other musical or social activities but rarely any full description of the instruments which were at the centre of their professional activities. There are stories of personal tragedies as in the unexplained suicide by arsenic of Mr. Thomas, organist of Crowan[2], or the untimely deaths of the young organists at Penzance, William Sholl (1820) and Launceston, William Putten (1824). Sholl—a native of Truro—first appears at the age of 19 advertising private music teaching and instrument tuning and repairs from his home in Rosewyn Row, Truro. By 1816 he has added the position of organist at Penzance to his teaching for

> private pupils or schools in Truro, and any Towns in vicinity or West. The flattering approbation of several of his friends, as to the progress of his Pupils, induces him to pay the strictest attention to their advancement in so noble a science.[3]

Less than four years later the same journal reported his death.

> Died at Leghorn, on the 1st instant, Mr. William Sholl, aged 28, where he went for the benefit of his health. He was organist at Penzance, and native of this town [Truro]. His modest unassuming manners procured for him friends in every situation of his chequered life; and although distant from his relatives and friends, it is no small consolation for them to know, that his last hours were softened by the kind attention of strangers. [*WB* 24 March 1820]

The musician with sufficient expertise, energy—and good health—to manage the continual round of private lessons, instrument maintenance and professional duties often made a significant contribution to the musical activities of his neighbourhood. The part played by the singing master Swaffield to choral music in the St. Austell region has already been discussed and several organists had a similar impact upon their communities. Distinguished local patrons at Bodmin, George Hart of Lanhydrock and James Laroche, made an important gift to the fine Parish Church in 1775 of a new instrument built by Byfield; over the years both the church and the town benefited from the presence of a professional musician.[4] An advertisement in the *Royal Cornwall Gazette* on 3 October 1801 for applications to fill the vacancy of organist—to be addressed, as most vacancies for organists were, not to the vicar or parish council, but to the Town Clerk—stressed both the 'great Salary' on offer and the opportunities for additional teaching, and a similar entry twenty years later boasted the challenge of the appointment.

The organ is an excellent one, and stands in one of the finest Churches for music in the West of England. None but persons of ability and good moral conduct need apply. [*WB* 27 April 1821]

The successful candidate on this occasion was J.L.Lutman who was soon to describe himself as 'Professor of Music and Organist'.[5] The town which had a long tradition of Balls and assemblies soon possessed under Lutman's direction an amateur concert society 'which from the talents of the performers bids fair to equal any in the county'.[6] For his first concert Lutman drew upon local talent of 'Gentlemen Amateurs' to provide 'a highly respectable [orchestra] complete in every part'.[7] Within the next few years he was drawing upon regional professional support including Joseph Emidy, Sharp, the Falmouth organist, the master of the Cornwall band, singers from Exeter and the young vocalist Charles Frederick Hempel, the son of the Truro musician who had built a high reputation for his performances and who was to pursue a successful career as musician in his adult life.[8]

In 1816 the Town Clerk's Office at Helston placed an advertisement for the vacancy of the post of organist at a salary of £40 *per annum*; an attraction of the post was the opportunity for additional teaching work as 'a music master is much wanted in the Town and neighbourhood'.[9] In the 1820s Helston enjoyed a flourishing amateur concert society drawing upon local performers and county professionals—including Joseph Emidy—under the direction of Roger Faning, organist at the Parish Church.[10] In Falmouth, as we have seen, the active concert life of the early years of the century saw a revival after the period of decline through the energies of Mr. Sharp in the 1820s. In addition to his organist duties Sharp also ran a musical academy, teaching the pianoforte, violin, flute and 'cello and a lengthy advertisement for the sale of his household goods following his relinquishing his post in 1825 gives a fascinating picture of the resources used by a professional musician of his day. In addition to the premises of the academy 'fitted up with great taste and at considerable expense', a vast quantity of music was advertised for sale including the classical masters—Handel, Mozart, Haydn and Beethoven—as well as contemporary figures such as Weber, Cramer, Kalkbrenner, Hummel, Pleyel and Moschelles. The selection of composers indicated a taste which was completely in touch with the most modern works of the age. Household furniture and material appropriate for a teaching establishment—desks, lecture board, stools and ruled slates—was supplemented by four Broadwood pianos and others by unnamed makers 'all selected by an Amateur of celebrity and particularly distinguished by mellifluence', two cocoa and box wood flutes, a violin and a large Aeolian harp. The list concludes with twenty feet of railing and posts![11] Perhaps Sharp's successor proved less effective than his predecessor for in 1826 the organist was instructed to 'obey the orders of the minister for the time being as to all singing, chanting and playing in the church'.[12]

No account of the parish organists at Falmouth would be complete without a reference to Edward Kendall who occupied the post from 1760 to his death in 1792, aged sixty six, when he was succeeded by his son. In 1775 he published *Six Voluntaries for the Harpsicord or Organ by different masters*. The title page of this volume, printed in London, indicates that these pieces were 'never before Printed'; as the individual items have never been identified as the work of any other composer there has been speculation that they might be the work of Kendall himself. Such modesty is a rare attribute, especially upon a title page and the speculation must be treated with circumspection. The voluntaries, whether that are Kendall's own composition or not, are an interesting example of the sort of music which he must have performed during the course of his work at the church. The six pieces follow a similar pattern of a slow introductory section leading to an extended quicker movement. In style they are similar to many other works circulating at the period, echoing the idiom of Handel's keyboard music and full of popular eighteenth century harmonic devices such as sequence and suspensions; they also make frequent use of echo effects. Though the publisher advertised the works as for 'harpsicord or organ', they are clearly conceived for the latter, not only by including indications of appropriate organ stops, but in the harmonic reliance upon sustained notes which would be impossible to create effectively on the harpsichord. Though of no great originality the pieces have a vigour and charm which merit occasional performance; they are accomplished in technique and show touches of imagination in the use of contrasts of register and colour possible on the contemporary organ.

It is however the organ and organists of St. Mary's, Truro, which are the best documented. The record of the instrument itself is particularly fully described due to the efforts of Dr. Richard Taunton, physician, amateur historian and—possibly—amateur musician, who assembled a large manuscript history of the town, intended for, but never achieving, publication. This collection, preserved in the Library of The Royal Institution of Cornwall, is particularly valuable in that Taunton gathered the opinions of experts in assembling his material and, when collecting information about the music of the Parish Church, consulted the organist, Charles William Hempel, who described the instrument in some detail. A further description, also based upon the first hand knowledge of Hempel was published some thirty years later by E.Spry in the twenty second *Annual Report* of the RIC (1840). Thus we have two almost first hand accounts by a professional performer of what was recognised as a particularly fine instrument, and one which survived the demolition of the church to serve as the instrument in the temporary building used as a church whilst the new cathedral was being erected; the organ eventually found a place in the St. Mary's aisle of the Cathedral and still survives.

The money for the purchase of the organ was advanced by William Lemon who funded a major rebuilding of the church in the 1750s; the refurbishment included the erection of a gallery with pews open to rent, the income from which reimbursed the initial grant. The instrument was built by Byfield, a distinguished organ builder who, in addition to the Bodmin instrument, was responsible for organs at St. Mary Redcliffe, Bristol, Christ Church Cathedral, Dublin and Archbishop Tenison's Church, Regent Street, London.[13] One account tells that the Truro instrument was originally built for the Chapel Royal though it did not suit the situation: the instrument as described at the beginning of the nineteenth century was of three manuals, a great organ of ten stops, a swell of six and a small choir of three. As was normal in eighteenth century organs there was no pedal board, though two pedal stops operated the swell mechanism and the kettledrums. Fine though this instrument was, in Hempel's opinion it had some limitations of range which could be remedied by expenditure of some fifteen guineas. By 1840 these modifications had taken place though the additions did not match the quality of the original. A pedal board had also been added following the raising of an £80 subscription; this improvement was of 'vast importance to the efficiency of the instrument as an organ without double diapasons is as incomplete as an instrumental concert without a double bass'. The high quality and musical standards of the instrument had been maintained and it would serve as 'a model for organ builders of the present day who seem to prefer external decoration to perfect workmanship and so sacrifice that richness of tone possessed of old organs'.[14]

Only three musicians occupied the post of organist at St. Mary's from the installation of the organ in the 1750s to the retirement of Charles William Hempel in 1845. Before the installation the standard of the amateur singers—'many Gentlemen (without any profession)'—was excellent according to reminiscences collected in Taunton's notes:

> They not only had very fine part singing but some even sang solo anthems—
> But on the erection of the organ they appointed a *bungling* Performer as
> Organist who had been a dancing master named Harrison, who altered the

mode + spoild the singing until the late organist Mr.Bennet[t] (whatever might be his mistake in the choice of Voluntaries) laid the foundation for the present mode; . . .

Charles Bennett, who succeeded the incompetent dancing-master Harrison in 1764, occupying the position as organist until his death in 1804, was an interesting character, known throughout the town for his musical skill and his sociability. He had been blinded in an accident with an exploding gun in childhood but this did not apparently hamper his musical development. He was a pupil of John Stanley (1712–1786) who was also blind though this did not prevent him having a successful career as organist and composer, eventually succeeding Boyce as Master of the King's Band of Musick in 1779. Bennett undertook teaching engagements throughout the county in his younger days. He wrote poetry, published a set of twelve songs and a cantata, and wrote music for the organ. His obituary in *The Royal Cornwall Gazette* (14 April 1804) records that he had 'a coruscant wit and convivial temper', a fondness for horticulture, recognising plants and weeds by their shape and scent, a taste for whist, distinguishing the cards by marking the pack with needle holes and a good memory, especially for long outstanding debts! In spite of his youthful accident, he retained a love of fireworks. Though his contribution to raising the standards of music in the church were admired, his love of lively organ music brought him into regular conflict with the church authorities. During his curacy at St. Mary's, the Rev. Richard Polwhele recalls that the Rev. Charles Pye, rector between 1764 and 1803

> often took Bennet[t] the organist to task, for playing 'jig voluntaries'. 'Why Bennet[t] (he exclaimed one Sunday), you will set all the congregation a-dancing'.[15]

Bennett's *Twelve Songs and a Cantata* was published in London, probably in the 1760s or 1770s and is a rare example of secular music composed by a Cornish musician in the period. It belongs to a tradition of secular song very popular in the later eighteenth century, echoing the fashionable music of the London Pleasure Gardens. Many regional composers contributed their own variations on the genre and Bennett's work which is no better nor no worse than many other composers' music, is relatively unusual in offering a full instrumental accompaniment, not simply a figured bass for a keyboard instrument and 'cello for the majority of items in the collection.

The poems upon which the songs are based inhabit a world of fashionable classicism; they are peopled by swains and nymphs, living 'sequester'd in lonely vales', where Phoebus marks the passage of day and Diana of night, where nightingales and turtle doves sing mournful songs of love and where Damon and Amelia, and other pastoral characters pursue their games of love. Such language may be conventional and dated, but there is a wit, charm and grace in the poems; society may have channeled its harmless flirtations and social relationships into the poetic conventions of the day, but the poems provide an ideal framework for sociable and elegant music. The pastoral too often has a twist in its tail, linking the abstract shepherds and shepherdesses to contemporary society with a sly humour.

> Ye swains did ye see e'er a Fair
> Trip carelessly over yon Mead;
> With ringlets of soft Flowing Hair
> And Garlands of Flow'rs on her Head.
>
> With Heav'n in her Aspect and Eye
> Her Cheeks like the blush of a Rose,
> Her Lips of the Cherry's deep die
> Her Breast Virgin Lilies compose
>
> She fill'd me with Love, and Surprize,
> For sure like a Seraph she sings,
> I'd ha'swore she had dropt from the skies,
> But did not observe she had wings.
>
> Some thought it was Venus th'Queen,
> With those I cou'd almost agree,
> So lovely her Air, and her Mien
> 'Twas certainly Emma or She.

[Song X; p.21]

Within the conventions, a lady poet, Miss Pitfield, can gently rebuke too ardent a suitor, as in the conclusion of 'O think not Damon':

> Thus soften what we can't redress
> This my request approve
> Let me in thee, the Friend possess
> Tho' fate forbids thy Love.

[Song VIII; pp.16-17]

Bennett's music complements the naive charm of the words; in most of the songs the solo voice is framed by extended instrumental passages, generally for two violins and continuo bass. In the first song there are directions that a flute should double the voice, and, though no such indication is given for later songs, it may be a practice which the composer generally employed. One song, 'Sequester'd in a lonely vale', adds a viola part to the violins and continuo, and the eleventh song, 'The wakeful nightingale', evokes the birdsong imagery of the verse by adding to the strings two independent flute parts and a *flauto piccolo*, doubling the first violin an octave higher. The most ambitious work, the concluding cantata which consists of alternating recitative movements with three solo airs describing Diana transforming Actaeon into a stag as punishment for interrupting her bathing, uses the most varied orchestral accompaniment; two horns are added to the string ensemble in the final section as Actaeon, in animal form, is hunted and killed. Interestingly the instrumental resources used in the volume—two flutes, two horns and strings—correspond exactly to those represented in the sketch of the Truro concert in 1808, though the picture does not include a keyboard player, essential to the performance of the songs. Though some thirty years separate the publication of Bennett's *Twelve Songs and a Cantata* and the drawing, the similarity of resources are a further indication of the slow change in the composition of provincial orchestras in spite of significant changes in musical style.

The musical language of the songs is, like that of the poems, firmly based in the eighteenth century idiom. Dance forms such as the minuet and jig provide a framework for a number of the songs, and, in the cantata, Bennett utilises the *da capo* aria form familiar from opera, though the majority of the songs are in a simple strophic structure. When orchestral instruments are added to the harpsichord accompaniment, as they are in all but two of the songs, considerable use is made of thematic imitation between voice and instruments, and, where appropriate, images from the poems—echo effects, huntsmen or birdsong—are developed in the instrumental passages. Even though the majority of the recitative passages in the cantata are simple, there is one moment in the final recitative when Actaeon flees before the hunters' dogs when a violent gesture in the keyboard shows that Bennett had experienced, and learned from, similar illustrative passages in the recitatives of Handel and other eighteenth century composers. Above all, one can sense in two songs in particular—the final cantata and the jovial 'A Term full as long as the siege of old Troy'—Bennett's delight in jig-like rhythms which so upset Rev. Charles Pye in his playing of church voluntaries. It is perhaps symptomatic of the man that his testimony as a composer does not take the form of church music from which he earned his living, but of sociable, good natured secular music which, no doubt, delighted his friends in Truro in the last decades of the century.

Bennett's successor as organist was the Chelsea-born musician Charles William Hempel. Some account of his benefit concerts, his contribution to the Truro Harmonic Society and the festival of 1813 has already been given, but more details of his career are of interest. An autobiographical letter, written from Truro on 2 February 1824 to the 'Proprietors of the "New Biographical Dictionary of Musicians"' provides some interesting facts.[16] Born in 1777 Hempel was the eldest son of the Chelsea potters and crucible manufacturers, Carl Friedrich Hempel and his wife Johanna [nee Ruel]. Their names suggest recent German origins. His musical talents developed early, largely due to the encouragement of his uncle Augustus Frederic Christopher Kollman, a German-born organist, composer and theorist who settled in London in 1782, occupying the post of organist at the Royal German Chapel at St. James's Palace. Kollman spent much of his long career refining an innovatory theory of harmony and composition which he published in a series of essays; his nephew who was allowed to perform at the Royal German Chapel when only eight years old, credited his own knowledge of composition entirely to the work of his uncle. In addition to his musical studies, he was educated at a boarding school in Surrey,

> where those hours which others devoted to sports and idleness were by [me] him dedicated to music and drawing. In the years 1793–4 [I] he went on the continent principally at Leipzig and Dresden -when he [I] had the most enviable opportunities of cultivating the chief pleasure of his [my] life, *Music*. On his [my] return to London he [I] became acquainted with some of the most eminent professors, and [I] lost no opportunity of the improvement which such acquisitions afforded [me] him. He had at this time the honor of being introduced to the immortal Haydn. [whose works with those of Mozart I have long regarded as models of perfection and from which I have endeavourd to form my taste.] Various circumstances some years after this period induced [me] him to have recourse to music as a profession (which hitherto had not been the case) and a prospect of [my] him succeeding to the organ at Truro being held out to [me I] him he was in 1803 induced to quit the metropolis.[17]

What the 'various circumstances' were which caused Hempel to direct his career towards music must remain a mystery, as must be the reason for his decision to move to Truro in 1803. One can only speculate that a prominent figure in Truro society, recognising that Charles Bennett was approaching the end of his life, advised Hempel that a suitable vacancy for an organist would be available in the town in the near future; the young organist, as far as we know, had no existing contacts with Cornwall. Whatever the reason, it proved to be a good one both for the music of the town and for Hempel himself for he was to make a significant contribution to the musical life of the area for the next forty years. In May 1804 he was elected to succeed Bennett as organist at St. Mary's; the concert and ball for his benefit advertised in the *Royal Cornwall Gazette* on 14 May 1804 must have been his first professional appearance in the area.

During his early years in the county he appears to have combined two careers, for in the account of his wedding to the daughter of a Penryn surgeon at Kenwyn Parish Church, he is described as 'of the Cornish Bank' (*RCG* 12 March 1808) but little more than eighteen months later he announced his intention of earning his livelihood solely from music, an indication of his growing reputation in the area:

> Mr. Hempel announces that it is his intention immediately after Christmas next, to devote his time solely to the MUSICAL PROFESSION, and that he proposes extending his attendance on Pupils in the vicinity of Truro and the towns adjacent.

Hempel's annual benefit concerts, his reputation as a performer and composer and his contribution to musical activities became a regular feature of the pattern of events recorded in the local papers. As a composer, his church music was admired; an anthem 'which did honor to the musical talents and taste of that Gentleman' was reported in *The Gazette* of 28 October 1809, and Hempel must be the strongest candidate as the composer of the *Te Deum* which so delighted Madame Catalani and the other visiting professions at the Festival in 1813. He published an *Introduction to the Pianoforte*, announced in the press in 1822 and referred to in his letter to the publishers of the Dictionary and included a song, 'Thro Groves sequester'd', in his 1815 concert, but his secular music does not appear to have survived. It was in the field of church music that he concentrated his principal efforts; this was no doubt an integral part of his desire to raise the standards of the music of St. Mary's to the highest level possible. As his autobiographical letter states:

> *Sacred* music now became [my] his chief delight, and he has spared no pains in producing a choir, the performance of which is rarely to be equalled out of a Cathedral.

The four substantial collections of Hempel's church music are all undated, but internal evidence and details from his letter suggest that they all appeared during the 1820s. The dates proposed in the *Bibliotheca Cornubiensis*[18] for the two collections of psalms, 1805 and 1812, are almost certainly too early; Boase and Courtney also do not record the publication of Hempel's most ambitious publication, *Church Services and Anthems* dedicated to George IV, nor the pianoforte tutor. Hempel's own account of his publications specifies

> a volume of Church Services anthems and Psalms dedicated to the Bishop of London. This has been received with the most flattering applause and may come to a second edition. [I] He has also published an *'Introduction to the Pianoforte'* and has ready for the press a second edition of *'Twenty Sacred Melodies'* dedicated to the Earl of Falmouth.

Also almost ready for the press was a work upon which he placed great value;

> [But my] His next work, now also ready for the press, and which is honored by the patronage of the King will [I believe] probably eclipse his other publications [all that has gone before—and I hope be worthy of the high honor to which it is destined.]

His plans for a second edition of the music dedicated to the Bishop of Lincoln, together with his great expectations for his forthcoming work are reinforced by a news item in the *West Briton* on 12 January 1823;

> We learn with much pleasure, that Mr. Hempel's musical talents promise to rank him among the first composers of sacred music in this country. His late work dedicated to the Bishop of Lincoln, is gaining deserved celebrity—and his services are performed by some of the finest choirs in the Kingdom. A second edition of this work...will be published in the course of next week. We also learn that he has an entire new work of Church Services and Anthems in great forwardness, in which he had exercised his highest powers, and which will shortly have the honour of making its appearance under the patronage of the King.

The two editions of psalm settings, *Sacred Melodies Adapted to the Psalms of David*, are the least interesting of his publications. Dedicated to Viscount Lord Falmouth, they were, according to the title page 'selected and composed for the congregation of St. Mary's Truro'. Congregational singing of psalms, as the Preface states, quoting distinguished authorities, allows all to 'share in a most noble and edifying effect' and to join 'one of the grandest scenes of unaffected Piety that Human Nature can afford'. Hempel shares the opinion of Dr Brown, 'a very good judge of musical composition', that congregational psalm singing of a high standard would 'add greatly to the solemnity, dignity and beauty of our Public Worship'. To fulfil these high ideals and aspirations Hempel gathered together fifty psalm settings, arranged simply as treble and bass melodies with small notes to fill in the harmony; as such they are clearly designed for unison congregational performance with an organ, and are not suitable for choral singing in parts. Dynamic markings are added to the music, as are indications of trills and other ornaments; in itself this is somewhat unexpected as ornamentation is not generally a feature of unison congregational singing. Tempo indications are included and some—*con supplica e Pia, Largo assai e con supplica, Espressivo e con supplica*—display a colourful individuality. No less than twenty nine composers are identified, the majority dating from the late eighteenth century, but others, including Luther, Ravenscroft, Purcell and Handel—representing earlier periods of musical history. Hempel himself contributed thirteen of his own melodies to the collection. Because of the simplicity of texture and variety of contents the two volumes are of a very useful, practical nature and it is not surprising to find organists and church wardens amongst the list of subscribers.

The other two volumes, *A Morning and an Evening Service*, dedicated to the Bishop of Lincoln, and *Church Services and Anthems*, dedicated to George IV, are more substantial in every respect. Both are in full score for a choir with an independent organ accompaniment, and both make extensive use of solo voices to vary the musical texture. The format of both volumes is similar; each contains a full Morning and Evening Service, together with appropriate wordless chant melodies, and a selection of psalm settings and full anthems. The publication of *A Morning and an Evening Service* was subscribed to by organists and by five Bishops, those of Durham, Ely, Exeter, Winchester as well as the dedicatee. This is an impressive spread, suggesting that the composer's name was beginning to command attention outside Cornwall.

The quality of the music merits serious attention also; unlike Swaffield's *Twenty Five Original Melodies* Hempel's volumes are not merely of local interest, but indicative of a competent and imaginative composer. The two complete services show a skilful use of resources; one could point, for example, to the changes of texture for dramatic effect achieved by the use of *decani* and *cantoris* divisions of the choir, the alternation of solo voices and full choir and contrasting organ registrations in the *Te Deum* in B flat from *A Morning and an Evening Service* at the words 'Holy, Holy, Holy Lord God of Sabbaoth' and 'O Lord in Thee have I trusted'. The accomplished contrapuntal writing for full choir and the rhythmic and melodic variety of solo passages all contribute to the variety of textures which maintains interest throughout the music. One curiosity of Hempel's style, perhaps derived from Kollman's harmonic theories, is an occasional tendency to sudden and—for the period—violent harmonic changes of tonal centres for dramatic effect, often marking changes in mood between different sections of the text. In the *Te Deum*, for example, the music has reached the key of A flat and suddenly plunges into E minor at the words 'O Lord save thy people'. Within ten bars the key passes through A minor before twisting back to the home tonality of B flat. The effect is startling and is far removed from the chromaticism which is associated with much Victorian church music; it can only be seen as a dramatic attempt to bring the force of the words, and their meaning, to the listeners attention.

The four anthems of *Church Services and Anthems* are technically accomplished and imaginative. Many passages show a high degree of contrapuntal skill, such as the tenor duet, 'He appointed the moon' from 'O Lord my God, Thou art become exceeding glorious' where a canon builds to a powerful climax around a chain of suspensions; a similar fluency of contrapuntal writing is in evidence in the choral passages which are often built fugally around two contrasting themes, a procedure which allows Hempel to create extended passages of varied music and contributes to impressive climaxes. A good example of this device is the final section of 'Like as the Hart' which includes two such double subjects as well as incorporating a light textured soprano solo with delicate organ figuration at the words 'and upon the harp' before the final homophonic chorus. An equally powerful sense of musical imagery is apparent in the bass solo from 'O Lord my God' where, to the words

> Who layeth the beams of his chambers in the waters
> and maketh the clouds his chariot
> and walketh upon the wings of the wind

the driving unison energy of the organ introduction is intensified as the music opens up into more parts, with syncopations, sequences and a falling chromatic bass. The entry of the voice restores the stark unisons which prevail for much of the section, though more textural elaboration appears as the images of clouds and wings of the wind are reflected in the music.

It is unfortunate that modern taste has little time for the church music of the Georgian and Regency periods for the quality and imagination displayed in Hempel's music at its best merits a revival.

Hempel's social standing in the town as organist at the Parish Church was sufficient to allow him to occupy a house in Lemon Street.[19] Though Joseph Emidy's home in Charles Street was close in proximity to Hempel's handsome town residence, the contrast in social rank between the two houses illustrates clearly the disparity in status between the two musicians. Nevertheless it is surprising that there is no record that the two most accomplished musicians in Truro, living only a few hundred yards from each other and both active as teachers, performers and composers, ever collaborated in musical projects.

Hempel remained as organist until 1844. He died in London in 1853 at the age of seventy nine.

The position of the Hempel family in Cornish musical life was further strengthened by the talents of his son, Charles Frederick, born in 1811, who commanded a growing reputation as a boy singer. The young man's contributions to various concerts were invariably advertised as a key attraction. His local reputation reached its climax in a series of farewell concerts in July 1825 before he prepared to try his fortunes elsewhere.

> We understand that out little Cornish vocalist, Master Hempel, intends (prior to his departure for the Metropolis) to give a concert at Helston and Penzance. We sincerely hope he may meet with that patronage to which his superior talent entitles him. His rapid improvement in the art has excited the astonishment of all that have heard him; and when time and study have matured his judgement, he will, we have no doubt, attain to professional eminence of the highest order.[20]

It is not clear how long this absence from Cornwall lasted; six months after his farewell concerts he performed at an election dinner and ball;

> . . . glees and songs, those in particular executed by Mr. Charles Hempel, beguiled the passing hours, and on the whole we never witnessed an entertainment in which mirth, good humour, and social enjoyment more fully prevailed. (*RCG* 24 June 1826)

The hopes of the *West Briton* were perhaps a little over optimistic for the young Hempel was destined for a steady, though not brilliant, career in the musical profession. He settled in Truro to succeed his father as organist of St. Mary's in 1844. A Bachelor's degree in Music at Oxford (1855) followed by a Doctorate in 1862 provided academic respectability; he left Truro for Scotland in 1857 to become organist at St. John's Episcopal Church, Perth, a position which he held until his death in 1867.

The Taunton manuscript helps us to flesh out a little the bare skeleton of details related to the life of the organist in the early years of the century.

The organist's salary was £45 *per annum*, £30 from the parish rates and £10 from the corporation, the remainder being raised from the income collected from the seat lettings in the gallery. There was a restructuring of the musical parts of the Service after 1805 when Hempel introduced a new version of *Tate and Brady* psalms and the records show the occasional purchasing of new sets of psalm books and grants of modest sums from the parish and congregation to assist the support of the standard of singing. Bullock reports that by 1857 the choir consisted of only 'two paid tenors, and three unpaid boys', though a revival strengthened the choir, increasing by 1861 its numbers to eighteen boys, twelve 'lads' and men, all unpaid; the fine Byfield organ was in need of both tuning and repair, and a major restoration was undertaken in the following two years.[21]

There is clearly more to be discovered about the organisation, quality and standards of music in church and chapel in Cornwall. It is to be hoped that more of the music itself will be discovered; the illumination which even such a modest work as Swaffield's *Twenty Five Original Melodies* throws upon the bare records is considerable and, concealed among piles of papers in church buildings or private papers there may be more lost compositions, printed or in manuscript. What does emerge from the surviving records, music and newspaper accounts is only the tip of an iceberg; church musicians, organists and singing masters, professional and amateur, made an important contribution not just to the life of the establishment which they served. The best of them contributed to the educational and cultural development of their communities and provided a focus for the musical activities of their town or village. It is a story which merits telling in full and a profession which—often unregarded—deserves honouring.

PART FOUR

The Theatre

'A moral and instructive school of rational entertainment': The Theatre

Whilst the activities of the Harmonic societies were invariably built upon the enthusiasm of amateur members, supported where possible by assistance from professional musicians, the theatre in the early nineteenth century was entirely professional in its organisation and membership. A 'gentleman amateur' might willingly perform as an instrumentalist, or his wife or daughter as a vocalist, in a concert; to appear on the stage, however, was a very different matter. No doubt this reluctance was due in no small measure to the suspicion of immorality which had surrounded the theatrical profession throughout its existence; in spite of the constant references to the 'respectability' of the entertainment, the theatre and its personalities retained an aura of raffish danger and excitement. There is little doubt also that many members of respectable society who would happily attend a concert, ball or other assembly event, might well draw the line at being seen in the theatre, even as a member of the audience. Nevertheless professional theatre was available in Cornwall and, though its fortunes fluctuated from season to season, sufficiently popular to warrant extended regular seasons and purpose built theatres in Truro, Falmouth and Penzance, as well as shorter tours to other towns. It is not surprising that Truro and Falmouth were the two centres in which theatrical activities were most firmly based. In addition to the appeal to the local gentry and merchants, the cosmopolitan audience of naval and military officers and their families who perhaps had experience of play-going elsewhere would certainly look for similar entertainments in Cornwall. It is also salutary to realise that the inhabitants of early nineteenth century Truro and Falmouth had a considerably greater opportunity to visit professional theatre locally than their twentieth century descendants.

In spite of all the prejudice there was a spurt of activity in the building of new theatres in the provinces in the last quarter of the eighteenth century. Most of the building was undertaken by commercial enterprise rather than drawing upon public funds. The principal concern of the theatre managers was to accommodate the largest possible audience; architectural distinction was a low priority. Few of these buildings survive in their original form, though the facades of others remain. Truro's first purpose built theatre and assembly rooms opened at High Cross in 1787; in its early days it saw a memorable—and often recalled—visit from Mrs. Siddons. It was rarely to see again such distinguished performers, being usually occupied by touring companies which used the premises for short seasons. Gilbert describes the building as 'handsome' and notes that, 'by laying an additional floor over the pit', the theatre could be converted 'at the proper time of year' into the principal assembly room.[1] In addition to the public rooms there was an adjoining house which was to be let to an occupier prepared to provide services to the building. As an Advertisement in the *Sherborne Mercury* in 1790 stated:

> The taker will have the advantage of furnishing the Assembly with tea and coffee; and if taken by a publican great benefit may be derived from an attendance at the Theatre.[2]

The dual function of theatre and assembly room was unusual but sensible and practical. Truro could rarely support regular extended theatrical seasons, but purpose built assembly rooms were a real asset to the community. Like Gilbert most commentators also found the building handsome, elegant or neat, though Heard wrote in his *Gazetteer* (1817) that it possessed 'no exterior beauty', whilst recognising that the interior was 'judiciously contrived . . . to be either perfectly adaptable for scenic representations or easily converted into an elegant ball room connected with which are card-rooms and apartments for refreshments'. Though only the facade of the building now remains, decorated with charming relief medallions of Shakespeare and Garrick, it is hard to understand Heard's view as the building must have been one of the most attractive in the town, justifying the local pride in which it was held.

The building of Falmouth's new theatre caused some controversy in the early years of the century; during the season of 1802 which ran from February to early April, plans to redevelop the theatre by 'raising the roof'[3] were announced by Samuel Fisher, the actor-manager, who owned the building. The location of the building, however, caused some concern:

The Chapel and the Theatre will be so very close, that the music and hubbub of the Theatre will be distinctly heard in the chapel. At present, the nights of preaching, and of playing, are the same—Mondays and Fridays: we shall see which will give way.[4]

The 'new and elegant theatre' was first used during Fisher's 1804 season in Falmouth which included performances of Sheridan's *The Rivals* and the popular ballad opera *No Song no Supper*. Fisher continued to organise an annual winter season in Falmouth throughout the first decade of the century, blending classics such as *Romeo and Juliet*, *Hamlet* and *As you like it* with contemporary plays, operettas and farces. By drawing upon the bands of visiting regiments, he often attempted to match the taste of the Falmouth audience for military music and provide a wide spectrum of entertainment. The *Gazette* of 2 February 1805 congratulated

the manager on the respectable augmentation that has taken place in the orchestra by the assistance of several of the musicians in the North Devon band whose masterly skill and execution cannot fail of contributing much to the amusement of the audience.

Fisher was also eager to introduce novelties of every kind to vary the programmes; in March 1810 he presented a male voice quartet performing Masonic songs 'in full clothing emblematic of that noble order' following performances of *The School for Scandal*, and in 1809 he staged an 'opera' called *The Mountaineers* to demonstrate the skills of a tight-rope walker;

... he will exert himself in a manner particularly astonishing, particularly with Table, Chair, Bottle, Glass, Skipping rope, Hoop etc. he will also dance on the rope with two boys tied to his feet.[5]

Fisher also took his company on tours throughout the county, presenting short seasons in specially adapted premises; not only the larger towns enjoyed these visits, but the company even ventured occasionally to the Isles of Scilly. From 1806 however, he had larger plans afoot. A news item in the *Royal Cornwall Gazette* of 20 December 1806 announced that he was negotiating a summer season at the Truro theatre and hoping to be granted a licence from the magistrates. Fisher's first Truro season, running from late May to the end of July 1807 was 'very unprofitable'. The performances included plays by Shakespeare—*Hamlet, Richard III, Macbeth*—but it was the comic songs and novelty acts which gained the most enthusiastic reports in the *Gazette* ; a sketch entitled *Mr. Vanotiens; or Prince Hamlet with a cork leg, and his one-ey'd Queen Mother* attracted some applause, but the longest notice was reserved for the seven-year-old Miss Randell who gave a pianoforte recital at the beginning of the season; the writer was astonished

> to hear the most difficult Sonatas and Concertos played with an effect which could have graced the fingers of a Clementi or a Dussek—to see hands which can scarcely reach a sixth, execute the most chromatic passages, with a degree of brilliancy and rapidity which can only be met with in our most finished performers.[6]

The financial failure of the 1807 season drew an extended series of reflections from the *Royal Cornwall Gazette* which gives a fascinating picture of the problems faced by a provincial theatrical company in trying to attract an audience. Social order and class differentiation clearly caused some conflict, as did the strong nonconformist tradition whose supporters 'could not be persuaded that the theatre is a school of morality'. Summer was also an inopportune period for the theatre to present its attractions; genteel families were 'summering at Bath' or on the Cornish coast and those remaining would prefer a river walk to 'inhaling the oily fumes from the lamps of the theatre.' Above all, however, class distinction remained a major reason. The pattern of social life and entertainment was well established and play-going fell uneasily into the pattern:

> nor, till a great change shall have been affected in the manners of its inhabitants (a change by no means desirable) will Truro ever prove a profitable scene of theatrical speculation.
>
> The high order of its inhabitants, enjoying the advantages of a good education, and being in the habit of frequenting London and Bath, have too highly refined their taste for dramatic performances to relish fare of a provincial theatre. This the manager is not ignorant of, but he knows too, that were he to bring down the popular London actors (as he once did Mrs. Siddons) that part of the population which might be thus attracted, is not sufficiently numerous to balance the heavy sums which the dramatic luminaries of the metropolis have the modesty to exact.—It should be recollected also, that a powerful motive for visiting the theatre in larger towns, has but little influence here. Our *Elegants* have other assemblies, in which they are seen and admired by all the fashionable gallants who either reside in, or visit the neighbourhood, without being elbowed by those of an inferior class; they have their concerts and harmonics in summer, with the addition of dancing and card assemblies in winter, and elegant conversation parties throughout the year, and while the planets thus retire from the theatrical hemisphere, their satellites cannot be expected to appear in.[7]

Novelty acts continued to appear occasionally at the theatre, such as Signor Belzoni 'the celebrated Patagonian Samson' who combined his strong-man act with performances on the musical glasses 'which for sweetness of tone and harmony, excel all other instruments'[8], but Fisher's ventures in Truro were suspended for a period. As Heard was to write in his *Gazeteer* in 1817, theatrical seasons were normally presented by 'a migratory company of players' every three years. In 1810 the *Royal Cornwall Gazette* of 18 August reported that Fisher had

> opened a negotiation with Mr. Hughes, for the Truro Theatre, and with great probability of coming to an understanding. One cause of the general ill success of Truro Theatre has been the season—summer: and our winter assemblies having come to a natural death, will remove that obstacle to the Thespians occupying our boards at a more appropriate season.

The winter season appeared a greater success artistically and financially, though poor weather affected the first week's attendances.[9] The promoters, Hughes and Fisher, stressed their intentions to provide performances which included 'the most approved and fashionable London pieces . . . produced in regular succession' and to render the Theatre 'a moral and instructive school of rational entertainment'.[10] Ticket prices ranged from three shillings for a box, two shillings for the pit, to a shilling for the gallery, and each evening's entertainment included a full length play as well as songs, short farces and occasional novelty items: the company included a child actress whose performances normally merited special commendation:

> Little Pickle in the *Spoil'd Child* was all life, and her introduced Hornpipe, as the Sailor's boy, excellent.[11]

Musical items were perennially popular;

> Provincial theatres are seldom supplied with much vocal excellence, but in 'The Quaker', Palmer though no *professed* singer, was highly respectable [as] Lubin; his laughing song was remarkably good.[12]

A local 'young gentleman' introduced a song on one evening and a 'new castanet song' was presented by one of the company, Mrs. Windsor. As one would expect, it was upon the variety, acting and presentation of the main plays that the success of the season depended and Fisher had sought to combine traditional favourites—*The Merchant of Venice*, *The Rivals*, *She stoops to conquer*, *Othello* and *Macbeth*—with novelties, some with the promise of horror—*The Ghost, The Castle Spectre*—comedy—*The Jew, or a School for Christians*—or romance—*A Cure for the Young Heart*. Standards of production were clearly intended to impress even the most experienced theatre goer:

> [*The Africans*] was produced in a style of splendor far surpassing anything we have witnessed on the Truro boards.[13]

Fisher and his company continued their peripatetic existence throughout Cornwall; there are spasmodic reports of their activities and occasional rumours of further developments of theatre in the region.

> Mr. Fisher's party . . . are now playing with great applause to very crowded houses at Redruth. It is expected that a subscription will take place for building a commodious theatre.[14]

He also extended his activities into Devon: it was there that he died in 1816 and, in his obituary in the *West Briton* on 24 June, he is described as manager of the Totnes theatre. He had maintained his Cornish interests, however, for in the following March an advertisement offered for auction in Falmouth 'all that newly-erected Theatre and premises situate in Killigrew Street . . . lately occupied by Samuel Fisher, comedian, deceased'. It was perhaps indicative of the financial insecurity of the profession that the advertisement stresses that the premises could be converted into dwelling houses! The theatre in Falmouth did survive, though a revival of activities of the Truro theatre over the next few years resulted in it becoming more of an outpost of the company based in Truro; following the peace with France it appears that Falmouth as a centre of social activities, so flourishing in the early years of the century, was in decline.

Fisher's successor as principal promoter of theatrical events in Cornwall was Dawson, also an actor who specialised in comic rôles. Like Fisher he promoted extended seasons in the county, generally every three years, but he used the Truro theatre, not Falmouth, as his major base. Both theatres were refurbished and redecorated in preparation for Dawson's seasons; the proscenium in Truro was newly painted and

> the Theatre has been fitted up with every attention to comfort; and those parts which have long stood in need of the renovating pencil of the artist have assumed an appearance of taste and freshness which cannot fail to give pleasure.[15]

Winter seasons were generally preferred and, by the judicious choice of new and fashionable plays as well as established favourites and a large and varied company of players, Dawson gave every intention of countering the adverse comments which had previously hampered the success of earlier theatrical campaigns.

There are many indications that this strategy was successful: the first season at Truro in 1821 was 'better than we have seen in this Theatre for the last fifteen years'[16]; the success in attracting a wider audience than earlier seasons was noted:

almost every one is there—and every one who is there is delighted.[17]

Before the company moved to give their performances in Penzance, Redruth and Bodmin, an anonymous 'Admirer of the Drama' wrote on 23 March that this had been

the most successful Theatrical campaign that has ever been witnessed in Truro.

Attempts to revive the summer season in 1824 were less successful; poor attendances were again ascribed to the alternative delights offered during better weather. The anonymous commentator, 'Aristophanes', summed up the dilemma;

How is it, Sir, that the refined taste of the metropolis of Cornwall should not display itself on such an occasion as the present? . . . [the theatre is empty], deserted for the more enlivening landscape of nature.[18]

The controversy generated by an acrimonious dispute between the rival critics of *The West Briton* and *The Royal Cornwall Gazette*, reflecting the opposed political views of the two journals, may have contributed to the modest increase in audiences in the later part of the season for even *Othello* drew a 'much larger auditory than frequently falls to the lot of tragedies in Truro'.[19]

Summer seasons were not attempted again. Winter performances returned to the successful pattern of the 1821 campaign. In Falmouth door keepers had to turn away patrons for the theatre was full to capacity,[20] and, in the same year Truro saw the most exciting—and unexpected— performance of the age.

Much of the 1825 season in Truro was predictable: a child prodigy on extended tour had delighted the audiences, as he was to do in Redruth and

Falmouth, with his skill on the violin and ability, though only six years of age, to act 'the most arduous characters in our standard plays'.[21] Master Burke—'The Musical and Dramatic Phenomenon, and considered Wonder of the Age'—appeared

> the fairy image of a man; [and] displayed a precocity of talent and acquirements, of which those who have not yet seen him can form no adequate conception. He enters upon the stage without embarrassment, and maintains his self possession amidst thunders of applause . . . Master Burke led the orchestra during the performance of some favorite overtures in a style that was truly surprising.[22]

The main dramatic offerings of the season ranged from a new comic farce, *Deaf as a Post*, to Dawson's admired performance as Shylock in *The Merchant of Venice*; as was predictable, Shakespearian tragedy—in this case *Macbeth*—was not well supported;

> Let but a tragedy be announced, and those patrons of the house allotted to the more refined part of the community are deserted. Whether this be owing to the absence of a relish for the intellectual enjoyment, or a supposition that Tragedy cannot be effectively performed on Provincial boards we know not.[23]

The 'refined' audience, as well as the less discriminating members of society, had, however, an opportunity to experience one of the most talked-about theatrical events of the decade when Dawson's company presented Weber's opera, *Der Freischütz*, early in December.

Der Freischütz had created an astonishing success following its first performance in Berlin in 1821. The work, a *singspiel* combining spoken dialogue and extensive musical items, became the foundation of German Romantic Opera through its brilliant fusion of a stylised conflict of good and evil in a setting which combined naturalistic realism and the super- natural. Musically it presented a combination of directly appealing popular choruses with sophisticated, expressive arias, accompanied by a virtuosity of orchestration which opened up a new world of instrumental colour and which was to have an enormous impact upon every aspect of contemporary music. The opera is one of those rare works of art which combined immediate popular success, reflecting the direct tunefulness of the scenes set in the German countryside and the Gothic horror of the Wolf's Glen scene, with an appeal to a new generation of artists and composers who were tentatively experimenting with the new idioms of Romanticism.

Immediately following its Berlin performance it became one of the most popular works on the operatic stage throughout Europe.

It is characteristic of Dawson's policy of offering the most recent novelties that he produced the opera in Truro in 1825, only four years after its world premier. The *West Briton* reviewer on 2 December recognised that allowances had to be made in the performance of 'an opera too celebrated to stand in need of comment' but confessed himself 'astonished at the superior manner in which this piece has been got up'. He makes no comment on the music—a surprising omission, one would feel in the review of such a work—but commended the staging of the Wolf's Glen scene. The report in the *Gazette* which appeared a day later of 'that extraordinary and wild piece' is a little more analytical in its comments but displays an interesting national bias against everything foreign. Like the *West Briton* reviewer, he had anticipated problems in the staging with the lack of space and stage machinery in the theatre; however his fears were relieved by some good individual performances and the quality of the costumes; he even found some features deserving praise in the music:

> Of the music by Weber it has been pronounced impossible to speak too highly—it may be so—in the Overture there are certainly elaborate and difficult combinations of a novel and striking character, and the laughing and hunting choruses are beautiful: but we have listened to English music which in our unscientific ears has sounded more pleasing, however unfashionable it may be to say so . . . It is a true scion from the *German* stock, and like other exceptionable dramas imported from the same source yet successfully represented on the English stage, as a literary composition it has nothing to recommend it to the chaste and moral conception of a British audience.

Interesting though these comments are, they evade so many questions to which one would like to know the answer. Three central roles present great difficulties to the singers and would demand a high degree of expertise and sensitivity to be effective; presumably from his company Dawson had actors capable of undertaking the parts. Essential to a successful performance is the choral and orchestral contribution. The opera includes choruses for male, female and mixed voices and a reasonable number of singers would be required to make even a partial success of these items; as the company was never large, did Dawson employ additional singers for this work and, if so, from where did he obtain them? As we have seen, there was no amateur choral tradition upon which he could draw to supplement his actors, even if he could persuade such singers to abandon their natural suspicion of the theatrical profession and appear

on the stage. Yet it will be noticed that it is the choruses which are singled
out for special mention, so the problem must have been solved at least
partially.

Even more crucial to the success and atmosphere of the opera is the
orchestra. Weber used his orchestra with an imaginative brilliance, creating
one of the complex and difficult orchestral scores of its day. To perform it
properly would demand a professional group of players, far exceeding
anything which we know existing in the region. Even to attempt performance with a reduced orchestration—however pale a copy it may have
been of Weber's original—would have put a severe strain upon the
resources at Dawson's disposal. Yet both critics are silent, beyond re-
marking that the Overture, one of Weber's most imaginative passages,
contained 'difficult combinations of a novel and striking character'.

Everything leads one to suspect that the 1825 production of *Der Freischütz*
can, at best,have been a musically abridged version of the original: the
orchestral and choral resources and the vocal demands of the principal
parts could hardly have been matched in any provincial theatre. Nevertheless the work *was* performed and brought to Cornwall one of the most
popular works of the European stage shortly after its first appearance. It
is a situation which could not be matched today!

The critical rivalry between the writers of the *West Briton* and the *Royal
Cornwall Gazette*, centering around a few controversial personalities and
events, produce in the reviews of the 1827/28 season the most detailed
picture of the theatrical activities; a number of these controversies centered
around musical issues and give us important information to flesh out the
skeleton of earlier reports.

The company consisted of between ten and twelve principal actors, each
specialising in a particular type of role. Dawson himself acted as manager
and performed comic leads; his ability as a singer of comic songs was also
of benefit to the company as it could be called upon to restore order to a
restive audience. There were a number of occasions during this season
when this gift was specially called upon. Early in the season he had to
introduce unadvertised songs when 'malcontents' in the gallery caused a
disturbance. Dawson expressed surprise that—as was the custom elsewhere
—'peace officers are not stationed in the theatre' to prevent such occurrences.[24] His wife, though not a regular member of the company, made
occasional appearances, and his son played all the children, including the
'little genie' in *Aladin*. Mr. Howard, a new member of the company, was
'a first rate acquisition . . . he is never seen without giving pleasure', though
Mr. Miller was

a chaste performer ... but wants ease in his carriage—he delivers his text with correctness, which would be much improved by a little more animation.[25]

Two further gentlemen made regular appearances, one only in minor parts, but the other, Mr. Keppel, specialised in Shakespearian leads including Hamlet, Macbeth, Richard III and Shylock. Knowing the disinclination of the Truro audience's response to tragedy, these were not always advantageous parts to enact:

> *Hamlet* was performed, for the purpose we suppose, of introducing Mr. Keppel—it would certainly be for no other—for without him, the piece had better been left to slumber on the shelf.[26]

Mrs. Osbaldiston was usually entrusted with the principal female leads such as Lady Macbeth or the Queen in *Hamlet*, as well as comic parts: she occasionally sang but was not noted for her talent as a vocalist. On the other hand, Miss Campbell, after a nervous start, usually sang at each performance, either as part of her role, or in specially introduced songs. Her talent however seems not to have been supported by suitable technical accomplishment.

> Miss Campbell has greatly improved in her vocal attainments—but we cannot help repeating our advice that she would 'study music'. She always sings in tune—has a voice of high cultivation—but she wants manner—she wants finish.[27]

It was her collaboration with Mr. Penphraze who joined the company in mid season with a 'tolerable' performance of Lorenzo in *The Merchant of Venice*, which was the principal cause of controversy with the critics, and of disruption in the audience. Penphraze was a counter-tenor—a voice little heard outside the cathedrals choirs in the nineteenth century—and his unusually high vocal range caused a major rift of opinion between the rival critics and—one suspects—was the cause of much barbed amusement and ribaldry from a section of the audience. The critic of the *West Briton* whose earlier reviews show that he had—or thought that he had—a sufficient musical expertise to offer detailed advice to the actors, was enthusiastic about the new performer.

> ...we have not yet seen his equal on the Truro boards. His voice (a counter-tenor) is not very powerful, but possesses much flexibility and sweetness, and his studies have been properly directed.[28]

Initially the *Royal Cornwall Gazette* critic who equally enjoyed displaying his command of musical jargon concurred with his rival journalist. He agreed with the criticism of Miss Campbell's technique but, whilst recognising some skill in Penphraze, was generally guarded in his comments.

> Miss Campbell should limit her efforts for the present to the natural tones of her voice, more pleasing than any effect she can hope to produce by soaring into the regions of *falsetto*, from which she has not yet acquired the most happy method of returning . . .
>
> Penphraze sang that beautiful song 'Said a smile to a tear', in which he made some pretty turns; but we would advise this young actor to study, if he may be allowed the expression, *the emphasis of music*, a more distinct expression of the words, and to be less lavish of the *trill* and the *run*, of which he appears to be perfect master, in important passages of his songs.[29]

From this point critical opinion began to divide: the *West Briton* continuing in support of the singer, the *Royal Cornwall Gazette* casting increasing doubts about his masculinity; whatever qualities Penphraze might possess as a soloist, in duets with Miss Campbell the effect was ludicrous:

> Mr. Penphraze continues to delight all who possess a taste for higher refinements of the vocal art—his talent places him far above many who make much *noise* in the musical world. (*WB* 23 November 1827)

> Mr. Penphraze, it appears to us, is only *half* understood in Truro—he would never otherwise sing without an *encore*. We, however, seriously recommend him to study a more intelligible enunciation. (*WB* 7 December 1827)

> [the duet was] an abortive attempt. Miss Campbell might have succeeded but for the strange tones and ludicrous gestures of Penphraze, which produced a sensible effect on the risible muscles of the audience. Why was not *Miller* sent on to sing the second [part]? His manly *English* voice would have been more suitable for this favourite duet, and better supported the lady. (*RCG* 5 January 1827)

Even the *West Briton* could find 'nothing flattering to announce' about the singing on this occasion. Another duet later in the season produced a similar response from the *Gazette*:

> It is much against the lady to be so matched; their voices will never harmonise. She executed her part in good style, but the lower notes of her companion scarcely reached the side boxes, and his upper notes defy description. He should sing *alone*, when he may rise into *alt* or *super alt* if he pleases, *hat* and

all, and enjoy his shake ad libitum, so we have no more duets. (*RCG* 12
January 1828)

By now critical rivalry was hardening as the *West Briton* reported on the
same performance:

It was really very well sung. Miss C. never displayed her vocal talents to so
much advantage, and Mr.P. gave his part with much sweetness. (*WB* 11
January 1828)

The aspersions against the unfortunate Penphraze's masculinity were
becoming more pointed and the views of his supporters more contentious.

Penphraze enacted *Count Basset* with his *usual ability*—could it be possible
that the sprightly Jenny was in danger from such a suitor?—but enough—our
prescription it seems disagrees with this choleric patient, who has much to
learn and to forget, before he will become even a tolerable actor. (*RCG* 19
January 1828)

We recommend Mr. Penphraze, not withstanding the jeers to which he has
been subjected, by a small part of the auditory, to cultivate his talent with
assiduity—to study music, and, with a manly contempt of his enemies, firmly
cherish the hope that his future fame will ere long cause them to regret the
endeavour to crush the aspirings of a real, though unappreciated, talent. (*WB*
18 January 1828)

With the advantage of a day's delay in publication, the *Royal Cornwall
Gazette* found opportunity to have a final word on this controversy;

With regard to the encomium pronounced upon his voice and singing by a
neighbouring critic—*chacun à son metier et son goût*—we can only repeat that
the effect of all that is ascribed to him when he sings in conjunction with
another is lost upon the *million*, this scientific judge himself being perhaps
the only *one* in that number who is sufficiently *refined* to enjoy it. (*RCG* 19
Jan. 1828)

What is clear from these reports is that things had begun to go wildly
astray within the company: the *West Briton* had already suggested that
Truro, in spite of its 'liberality towards the Drama', had neither the size
nor the population to support a season of such length.[30] However much
Dawson might have appreciated the early publicity ensuing from the
controversy—after all, no publicity is bad publicity if it sells tickets—he

cannot have been content that, on the evidence of the reports, dissension was now present among the company itself, especially in the orchestra. The audience disturbances early in the season had caused Dawson to step in and interrupt the advertised programme with some comic songs to settle the restiveness. The tension had also resulted in a number of reports which stressed the uplifting tone of the theatre and the high moral rectitude of the company:

> Mr. Dawson's company . . . are a well behaved and so far respectable class of performers who indulge in none of the immoralities ascribed to players. In a place like Cornwall where the prejudice, from the above causes, may be said to be strong, this is much in their favour.[31]

There was also news that a rival company had ventured into the county, which must have disturbed Dawson in threatening his livelihood.

> The Launceston theatre, recently fitted up, has opened by a company of players under the management of Mr. Hillington of the Exeter theatre. We have not space to notice this performance; nor can we imagine that the taste for theatrical amusements in Cornwall is so strong that two rival companies can exist with any fair prospect of success.[32]

All these factors encouraged Dawson to ensure that his season was as successful as possible, in spite of the controversies. Much more than in any other season he concentrated on strengthening the musical element of the evening' entertainment. Militia bands were introduced on a number of occasions. In November Sheridan's *The Rivals* was performed to a full house under the patronage of members of the Hare Pie Club and 'a military band attended in the orchestra, and contributed its full share to the amusement of the audience'.[33] A similar attraction was provided in early December when Lord Falmouth patronised a performance of *The Soldier's Daughter*, and in January, the Yeomanry Band added 'several martial airs with much precision and effect' to the evening's entertainment.

The introduction of bands, attractive as they may have been in their own right, appear to have served the purpose of compensating for growing problems in the orchestra; as orchestral playing is rarely mentioned in the reports of other seasons, we may assume that, in 1827, the problems were much more apparent than usual. As early as October the *West Briton* reviewer makes a slighting reference to the musicians. A performance of *Aladin* demanded resources of orchestra and scenery which would stretch any country theatre.

with respect to the orchestra, we can only say we have no room to waste criticism on it.[34]

A week later, possibly in response to complaints from the musicians, the reviewer clarified his views further:

> We shall be happy to notice the orchestra differently from our last, when *they feel their own importance* in such an establishment—our attack was not levelled at individual talent.[35]

By early November the reason for the disquiet was becoming focussed on the disruptive leader of the theatre band.

> On Monday our worthy Mayor patronised the performance, on which occasion our military band was stationed in the pit, and considerably atoned for the *want* of music elsewhere ... We cannot refrain from reproaching [Dawson's] orchestra. There is real talent in it which is past by—and a country-dance scraper elevated to a situation wholly foreign to his powers—why are these things not better arranged?[36]

The *Royal Cornwall Gazette* was equally concerned at the low orchestral standards, complaining that the singers' progress must be inhibited until 'the orchestra will try to play in tune.'[37] In its final review of the season the *West Briton* reverted to the question of the leader; earlier in the season the critic ascribed part of Penphraze's problems to the open hostility from the leader of the orchestra. This hostility was directed not only to the singer—where he had some support from a section of the gallery—but also at the audience itself.

> Reverting to the orchestral leader, we cannot help asking him this very simple question—whether, on any future occasion, his having the dread of catching cold, it would not be more respectful toward the audience, were he instead of wearing his hat in the orchestra, to substitute, say, a caxon—a tie—a bob—or even a Welch wig![38]

The account of the controversial season of 1827/28 gives us the most vivid picture which we have of the musical activities in the theatre. It gives a picture of ambitious, if often imperfectly executed, vocal ornamentation, of ballads and comic songs, being introduced on every possible occasion and of the importance of instrumental music—either from a military band or the pit orchestra—contributing to the evening's entertainment. Even from these details, however, we cannot determine how many musicians normally made up the orchestra, nor where they came from. It is possible that the leader, the country-dance fiddler who kept his hat on, moved with the company to different engagements, and it is quite likely that Dawson employed a small group of musicians as part of his permanent company. He may have also engaged local professionals to strengthen his group on occasions. Is it possible that Joseph Emidy occasionally supplemented his income from theatrical work? There is no evidence that he did, but it must be remembered that he had spent part of his early life as violinist in an opera orchestra in Lisbon; that sort of experience was unique among musicians in Cornwall. There is also the intriguing reference to 'a real talent' passed by in the orchestra who could more competently perform the duties of leadership. It is a question which cannot be answered, but one which is worth considering. Joseph Emidy's career as a musician was very different from his other professional contemporaries in Cornwall; most of them received part of their income as church musicians, supplemented by private teaching and occasional benefit concerts. For Emidy there was no professional contact with a church and his living was derived from teaching, repairs and tuning, attending balls and concerts; it would not be beyond the realms of credulity if occasional work in the theatre did supplement this precarious livelihood.

EPILOGUE

The Lost Composer

Joseph Emidy's presence flits like a ghost through the events which are described in these pages. Without a portrait or personal document connected with him, relying on two personal memoirs of those who knew him and heard him play, and on the brief newspaper accounts of his activities, his presence lacks any real substance. Only his grave provides concrete evidence of his existence, and the secrets of that remain silent. The documentation of his early life will probably always remain a mystery; the records pertaining to a single slave—and a child at that—amongst the many thousands who were torn from Africa to live their lives in foreign countries do not exist. The mystery deepens in Lisbon; how did a youth of his background develop his remarkable talent—and there is no doubt that it *was* remarkable—and progress so far in an alien culture? Moreover, how was he—a slave—allowed to develop this talent even in a society which, like Portugal, offered less oppressive treatment to slaves than many others? How did he get his new identity and name? It is only when he comes into contact violently with the British Navy that we can begin to know something of the events which he experienced. Even to these events—such as the dramatic rescue of the company of the *Dutton* or the terrifying circumstances of the wreck of the *Droits de l'homme*—he remains a silent witness. The rebuilding of a new life for the second time in Cornwall, his marriage, growing family and the professional work which he undertook, are a little better documented but offer no real insight into the nature of the personality which could survive the traumas of the early years and create a life which—considering all the problems—appears to have been successful. A novelist might be able to penetrate more deeply into the mind and creatively imagine the thoughts and motivations which allowed him to achieve some equilibrium, but no novelist, I suggest, would dare to create a story so bizarre or implausible as the life of Joseph Emidy.

Fate still had a final blow for him. The driving force which appears to have carried Joseph Emidy through these years was his love of music and determination to progress both as a performer and composer. Throughout his years in Cornwall there is evidence of new compositions being performed and presented in local concerts. Cornwall was not, as we have seen, the most propitious environment for a composer to work; few predominantly rural communities would have been in the early nineteenth century. No amount of local support and amateur enthusiasm could compensate for the scarcity of other professional musicians, the lack of regular concert series or the opportunity for performance of his music at the highest level. Only in the major centres of music making such as London or Bath could a composer hope to find the resources which could support his work. Even in London, few English composers of instrumental music established a reputation in the early nineteenth century, in spite of the popularity of orchestral concerts. The most popular and frequently performed composers were foreign, notably Haydn and Pleyel, who had consolidated their reputations abroad by spending extended seasons in England. No English musician could rival their success and few attempted to do so. The principal market for English music was the opera house, theatre and church and, as far as we know, Emidy never wrote music for these outlets. In spite of the obstacles, however, there was one attempt to promote Emidy's music on the national scene.

James Silk Buckingham's understanding and sympathy for Emidy's situation was reflected in the prominence which he gave to the young African's story in his *Autobiography*; it was also shown in a more practical terms during the composer's life time when he attempted to interest the most influential impresario of the age, Johann Peter Salomon, in advancing his career. The German born Salomon had been resident in London since 1781; though a brilliant violinist, he increasingly devoted his activities to conducting and promoting concerts. In the series of subscription concerts which commenced in 1788, he brought to London international artists of the highest calibre. The highlight of his activities were the two extended visits to London of Joseph Haydn in 1791/92 and 1794/95; these seasons had a profound effect not only upon the London audiences, but upon the final phase of Haydn's career itself, stimulating him to compose not only the twelve *London* symphonies which he introduced during the two visits, but to turn his attention to large scale choral works on his final return to Vienna. Salomon was later one of the founder members of the Philharmonic Society of London, leading the orchestra for its first concert in March 1813. His death, following a riding accident in 1815, drew many statements of regret from throughout the musical world. Buckingham's approach to Salomon was a shrewd move; if there was any chance of interesting a national audience in the music of the unknown foreigner, Salomon's concerts would provide the ideal platform.

Emidee had composed many instrumental pieces, as quartetts, quintetts, and symphonies for full orchestra, which had been played at the provincial concerts and were much admired. On my first leaving Falmouth to come to London—about 1807,—I brought with me several of these pieces in MS., to submit them to the judgement of London musical professors, in order to ascertain their opinion of their merits. At that period Mr. Salomans [*sic*], the well-known arranger of Haydn's symphonies as quintetts, was the principal leader of the fashionable concerts at the Hanover Square Rooms. I sought an interview with him, and was very courteously received.

This is a very important statement. At the date when Buckingham says that he took Emidy's manuscripts to London, only one composition by him had been named in the newspaper reports. This was the violin concerto which Emidy performed at his first Falmouth concert in 1802. Buckingham indicates that there was a much larger body of compositions than we could have possibly have known from any other source. These works, moreover, must have all been written since the young man was abandoned in Falmouth by Pellew. It is inconceivable that he would have been carrying music with him when he was kidnapped in Lisbon, and highly unlikely that he could have found opportunity to compose whilst held aboard *The Indefatigable*. In addition to building teaching and performing contacts, to bringing up a young family, Emidy found the opportunity and motivation to compose a significant number of works. Buckingham's narrative continues:

I told him the story of Emidee's life, and asked him to get some of his pieces tried. This he promised to do, and soon after I received an intimation from him that he had arranged a party of professional performers, to meet on a certain day and hour at the shop of Mr. Betts, a musical instrument maker, under the piazza of the Royal Exchange, where I repaired at the appointed time, and in an upper room a quartett, a quintett, and two symphonies with full accompaniment were tried, and all were highly approved.

Though Salomon was sufficiently impressed to suggest that Emidy should come to London to give a concert, Betts and the others felt

his colour would be so much against him, that there would be great risk of failure: and that it would be a pity to take him from a sphere in which he was now making a handsome livelihood and enjoying a high reputation, on the risk of so uncertain a speculation.

To show their admiration, a subscription was raised by the musicians, but no further attempt was made to bring Emidy and his music to London. Perhaps Salomon and his circle's apparent concern not to disrupt Emidy's life may also be interpreted as a comment on the standard of music, which they did not feel would be acceptable to London audiences, but at this distance one cannot be sure. There can be little doubt, however, that it was his knowledge of Emidy and his gifts which was one factor in forming the anti-slavery stance of his young admirer:

> these facts . . . offer another splendid proof of the utter groundlessness of the fallacy which supposes the negro intellect to be incapable of cultivation, or arriving at an equal degree of excellence with that of the whites, if placed under equally favourable circumstances. With the same advantages as were enjoyed by most of the great composers of Europe, this man might have become a Mendelssohn or a Beethoven: but as it was, it was the achievement of extraordinary perfection, in spite of a thousand obstacles and difficulties.

The failure to advance Joseph Emidy's career as a composer must have been regarded as a set back both by Buckingham and Emidy himself, but he continued to compose new works during the coming years. The details of the new works however must be approached with some care; as we have seen, Buckingham's account reveals that Emidy was much more prolific than we could have known from the surviving records, so the four, or possibly five new works of which we know may only represent a proportion of all Emidy's later music.

In 1808, as part of a concert to celebrate the king's birthday, Emidy played a violin concerto 'composed by him purposely for the occasion' and, two years later, a 'Concerto and Rondeau' was well received by the *Royal Cornwall Gazette*. There is no way of knowing whether this refers to two independent works, or whether the Rondeau was a movement of the Concerto. No new works are recorded until the 'Concerto for the French Horn' announced for the concert in Truro in December 1821. The final reference to new music occurs in a report in the *Gazette* on 2 April 1818.

> We understand that Mr. Emidy, the leader of our Philharmonic Society, has lately employed his talents in a rather novel manner for a professor of the violin, and has produced some variations on the subject of a Grecian air for the pianoforte, which evince not only a correct taste but considerable judgement, as regards the nature of the latter instrument. The production has been submitted to the inspection of competent judges, and highly commended. It is intended to publish it by subscription.

As with all the other compositions there is no later reference to

A view over Truro from the church yard of Kenwyn Parish Church, 1806. The artist's view point is close to the position of Joseph Emidy's grave.

Royal Institution of Cornwall

perfurmance nor any indication that the Grecian Air Variations were ever published.

Joseph Emidy died on 24 April 1835. According to the head stone on his grave he was in his sixty first year, though, as we have seen, he may have been a few years older. He was buried in Kenwyn Churchyard, Truro. Both local papers carried a short obituary, the *West Briton* of 1 May recording after a brief biographical note:

> His talents as a musician were of the first order and he was enthusiastically devoted to the science.

The *Royal Cornwall Gazette* of 25 April had carried a slightly longer notice of his death which has some strangely similar wording:

> His talents may be said to have ranked under the first order while his enthusiastic devotedness to the science has rarely been exceeded. As an orchestral composer his sinfonias may be mentioned as evincing not only deep musical research, but also those flights of genius which induce regret that his talents were not called into action in a more genial sphere than that in which he moved.

Other black slaves achieved unexpected careers—Pushkin's grandfather was a former slave who rose to the rank of general in the Russian army—and among Emidy's contemporaries there were those who fulfilled lives as musicians. Brindes de Salis, West Indian by birth, became court violinist to the Queen of Spain in the early nineteenth century, and George Bridgetower, for whom Beethoven wrote the *Kreutzer* sonata, was the half-caste son of an African father. In this respect Emidy's career is not unique. Fate however had the last word in the loss of all his compositions. Though the family lived in Truro for the next generation, it was not to survive longer in Cornwall. Some of Emidy's grandchildren emigrated to America in the later years of the century and continued in the family tradition by earning their living in touring circus bands. Though the American branch of the family survives, there is no knowledge of the fate of Joseph Emidy's music. This is not surprising; emigrants would have sufficient problems is carrying their own possessions to the new world, and a substantial pile of family papers, grandfather's music, would not have been among their priorities. As the family dispersed in England, as its members died and their homes were cleared, the fate of the manuscripts is also understandable. A pile of aging music paper, probably worn through use and damaged by damp, would not survive destruction easily. Unless the music has survived, lying perhaps forgotten amongst other old papers, Joseph Emidy's real memorial—his compositions—can never exist.

Perhaps Salomon and the other London musicians felt that, for contemporary taste, his compositions stood little chance of acceptance by the public; their rejection may have been couched in kindly terms to conceal a harsher truth—that the music was of poor quality. Today, however, a different set of criteria apply; the music *may* have been poor in quality and Emidy's achievement as a composer low, but, at this distance in time, his work can only be regarded as unique. Its uniqueness is not merely that it is associated with such a remarkable and unusual story, but that it would offer an insight into a fascinating blend of cultural conditions. In the late eighteenth and early nineteenth centuries successful orchestral music was largely composed within an international style which centred upon the idiom of the Austro-German composers. National idioms, regional musical dialects, played little part in this style although by the middle of the century there were signs that these conditions were changing. When Chopin captivated Parisian audiences with his recreations of Polish dance forms, when composers such as Glinka in Russia and Smetana in Czechoslovakia introduced folk melodies and dance rhythms into their compositions, musical nationalism began to have an increasing influence in the musical taste of the day. Music from the Iberian peninsula did not spread into the main stream of European music until the late years of the century, yet we know from Beckford's descriptions of Portuguese music how captivating it could be to sensitive ears. Did Joseph Emidy's music show any signs of this idiom? Did it more intriguingly even have echoes of his African youth? Without the music there is no way of knowing; none of the early commentators remarks upon such influence and speculation is unproductive. Whatever the quality of his work its disappearance denies us the opportunity of adding the final and potentially most exciting chapter in Joseph Emidy's story.

The Byfield Organ in St. Mary's Parish Church, Truro

Information drawn from MS notes (c.1800–1810) by Dr.Richard Taunton, currently held in the Library of the Royal Institution of Cornwall, and E.J.Spry's 1840 article on the church in JRIC.

Taunton MS
Byfield; builder
3 rows; range GG Bass to
   D in alt

Spry 1840
1750 Byfield; 'said to be bought for the Chapel Royal but did not suit the situation for which it was intended'. Hempel describes as 'rather contracted' range; G bass to D in alt
Short octaves

Lower row; Choir organ;
   3 stops
   flute
   15th
   stopped diapason

Choir; 3 stops 'very limited'
   diapason
   flute
   15th; 'quite useless;' intended to put in a dulciana in its place if the necessary fund can be raised, about £14'

2nd row; full or principal;
   10 stops
   principal
   open diapason
   stop diapason
   tierce
   12th
   15th

Great organ; 10 stops
Open diapason 'very superior quality'
stopped diapason, principal, 12th, 15th, tierce sesquialtra
Clarion*, trumpet*, cornet*
* 'not excelled perhaps in England' in the opinion of organ builders who have heard them

Taunton
Clarion
Trumpet
Cornet
sesquialtra

Spry

Swell; 6 stops

2 Pedals; right; swell
left; kettledrum

Swell set and pipes 'allowed the best in this organ, but it is much lamented that there are not base, or at any rate tenor notes in the swell which might now be added for about 15 guineas.

Swell; 'more complete'; 6 stops
open diapason 'rich and mellow'
'addition made to swell by Mr. Lincoln who carried it down to F below fiddle G. but the quality is not equal to the original'. Addition also made about 5 years ago by Buckingham (London) under the super-intendance of the great lover of musical science, the late Dr.Taunton; double diapasons added

1½ octaves of German pedals
Venetian swell and stop to connect great organ to pedals; cost £80 (subscription)— 'vast importance to the efficiency of the instrument as an organ without double diapasons is as incomplete as an instru-mental concert without a double bass'. (Cost £80, raised by subscription)

Byfield's reed stops are superi-or to most others but his ses-quialtra is too like the Cornet tone as Col. Lemon observes'

Organists salary: £30 from parish rates, £10 from the Cor-poration, £5 from rent of sit-tings in the gallery.

Information collected, as by Spry, from Charles Hempel, third organist at the church.

Reed work; 'mellow and beautifully round, and it may in this respect be considered as a model for organ builders of the present day who seem to prefer external decoration to perfect workman-ship and so sacrifice that richness of tone possessed of old organs'.

Keys; black and white
The organ is decorated by 'cherubims with trumpets'

APPENDIX B

Composers Mentioned in Concert Reports

Many of the composers whose names appear in the concert reports are now largely forgotten. This list gives brief biographical details of all the composers whose names are mentioned, with the exception of composers living in Cornwall whose work is discussed in the relevant chapters. A few names remain unknown even in such comprehensive volumes as *The New Grove*.

Arne, T.A [1710–78]	English composer of operas, ballads and instrumental music.
Beethoven, L [1770–1827]	German composer whose reputation was just beginning to reach England in the early years of the century.
Bishop, H.R [1786–1855]	English composer of stage and vocal music.
Callcott, J.W [1766–1821]	Distinguished English composer of glees and other vocal music.
Cherubini, M [1760–1842]	Italian composer of operatic, vocal and instrumental music, long resident in France.
Clementi, M [1752–1832]	Italian composer and keyboard player, a prominent figure in the development of the piano and its music; resident in England for much of his life.
Cimarosa, D [1749–1801]	Italian opera composer, particularly admired for his comic works.
Cramer, J.B [1771–1858]	Member of German family of musicians, particularly associated with the development of the piano. London was for much of his life the centre of his professional work.

Davy, J [1763–1824]	Exeter born composer of theatrical music and popular songs.
Dussek, J.L [1761–1812]	Czech pianist-composer, popular in his lifetime.
Eichner, E [1740–1777]	German composer and bassoonist, known for his instrumental music.
Griffin, G.E [1781–1863] ·	English composer best known for his instrumental works.
Guglielmi, P [1727–1804]	Italian composer of more than one hundred operas, as well as church music and some instrumental music.
Gyrowetz, A [1763–1850]	Czech composer, lawyer and diplomat. Composed in a wide variety of forms, including more than thirty operas and sixty symphonies.
Handel, G [1685–1759]	German composer resident in England for most of his creative life. His operas, oratorios and instrumental music had a dominant influence upon English taste throughout the 18th century.
Haydn, F.J [1732–1809]	Austrian composer whose reputation, confirmed by visits to London in the 1790s, made him the best known contemporary composer for English audiences.
Hoffmeister, F.A [1754–1812]	Dutch born composer who spent most of his working life in Vienna, composing prolifically, including 44 symphonies, a similar number of quartets, church music and singspiels.
Horsley, W [1774–1858]	London organist and composer of popular glees.
Jommelli, N [1714–1774]	Well known Italian composer of operas, church music, and instrumental works.
Kalkbrenner, C [1755–1806] or [1788–1849]	Distinguished German father and son, both well known as composers; the son was especially famous as a piano virtuoso.
Kent, J [1700–1776]	English organist, especially associated with Winchester Cathedral; composer of services and anthems for the Anglican church which were much admired.

Kozeluch, L.A [1752–1818]	The best known of a family of Czech musicians, who composed in a wide variety of forms, including 30 symphonies and 13 piano concertos as well as operas and chamber music. He succeeded Mozart as court-composer in Vienna.
Loder, J	Member of a large family of English musicians much involved in the promotion of Music Festivals.
Marcello, B [1686–1739]	Distinguished Italian composer, lawyer and poet, remembered for his church music and concertos.
Martini, G [1706–1784]	Italian composer, theorist and priest. He is probably best remembered as a teacher of strict counterpoint but he was a prolific composer, largely of sacred music.
Mazzinghi, J [1765–1839]	English composer of Corsican origins; known for his theatrical music, but also composed chamber music, piano sonatas and songs.
Meyer, P.J [1737–1819]	Alsatian harpist and composer; a pioneer in the use of the pedal harp, active in Paris from 1765 and settled in London from 1784.
Mozart, W.A [1756–1791]	Austrian composer; his reputation in England overshadowed by that of Haydn.
Paer, F [1771–1839]	Italian composer, particularly known for his operatic music.
Perez, D [1711–1778]	Spanish-Italian composer noted for his operas; for the last twenty six years of his life he was court musical director in Lisbon.
Pleyel, I.J [1757–1831]	Austrian composer, the pupil of Haydn, who lived in Paris from 1795. He visited London for the 1791-92 season, also the period of Haydn's first visit. A prolific composer, he was particularly associate with the development of the piano.
Portogallo, M.A [1762–1830]	Portuguese composer and conductor; a prolific composer of *opera seria* in Italian,

Romberg	comic operas in Portuguese and church music. A North German family of musicians, active at the end of the 18th. and beginning of the 19th. centuries, the majority of who composed in a variety of popular forms.
Rossini, G.A [1792–1868]	Italian composer whose operas were increasingly popular from 1815.
Sacchini, A,M.G [1734–86]	Italian composer, best known for his operatic music but who also composed sacred and instrumental works.
Shield, W [1748–1829]	English composer, much involved with theatrical music. His songs and ballads were very popular.
Stamitz, J.A [1717–1757]	The most prominent of a German family of musicians and composers who raised the reputation of the Mannheim orchestra to one of the finest in Europe of its period. He composed in most of the major instrumental forms.
Steibelt, D [1765–1823]	German pianist and composer, widely known throughout Europe both for his compositions and performances.
Stevens, R.J.S [1757–1837]	English organist and a popular composer of glees.
Storace, S [1763–1796]	English musician associated with theatrical work; he composed many stage works as well as some chamber music and songs.
Webbe, S [1740–1816]	English composer, best known for his glees.
Weber, C.M [1786–1826]	German composer who is one of the pioneers of the Romantic Movement. He composed orchestral music of distinction, though it is his operas which had the greatest impact upon the taste of the age.

NOTES

Prologue
1 *RCG* 8 February 1806.
2 William Beckford: *Italy with sketches of Spain and Portugal*; 1834 II, p.5.
3 *ibid*: p.10.
4 *ibid*: p.17.
5 'The private memoirs of Jonathan Couch': *JRIC* IX (1983), p.103.
6 *ibid*: p.103.
7 'A tour into Cornwall . . .' 1794; *JRIC* IX (1983), p.201.
8 James Silk Buckingham: *Autobiography* (London 1855); the account of Emidy which will be frequently referred to occurs between pages 165 and 172.

Chapter 1
1 D.P.Mannix: *Black Cargoes*; xiii.
2 D.Francis: *Portugal 1715-1808*, p.208.
3 W.Beckford: *Italy with sketches of Spain and Portugal*, 1834 II,p.240
4 *ibid*: p.243-244.
5 Francis: *op.cit*; p.122.
6 W.Beckford: *op.cit*, II p.78.
7 *ibid*: p.91.
8 *ibid*: p.82.
9 *ibid*: p.94.
10 *ibid*: p.60-64.
11 *ibid*: p.123.
12 *ibid*: p.253.
13 *ibid*: p.254-5.
14 *ibid*: p.86.
15 *ibid*: p.167.
16 *ibid*: p.73-74.
17 *ibid*: p.239.
18 *ibid*: p.71-72.
19 *ibid*: p.240.

Chapter 2
1 W.James: *The Naval History of Great Britain* 1837 I, p.199.
2 *ibid*: I p.96-99.
3 *ibid*: I, p.325.
4 Log book of Capt Ed. Pellew: *PRO ADM 51 1109*; 7 May 1795.
5 Parkinson, C Northcote: *Edward Pellew* p.128.

6 *PRO ADM36 13142.*
7 Throughout all the muster entries during Pellew's captaincy the name is invariably spelt in this way, except for two occasions when it appears as Emeda [July/August & September/October 1796 *ADM36 13143*].
8 N.A.M.Rodger: *The Wooden World: An Anatomy of the Georgian Navy.*
9 Documentation of *Mutiny on the Bounty* Exhibition, Greenwich, 1989; exhibition item 196.
10 W.R.Tuck: *Reminiscences,* p.18-20.
11 M.Lewis: *A Social history of the Navy 1793-1815.*
12 *ibid,* p.129
13 N.A.M.Rodger: *The Wooden World:* p.160-161.
14 London 1844; quoted by Lewis: *op.cit,* p.129.
15 N.A.M. Rodger: *The Wooden World:* p.125.
16 *ADM51 1171* Saturday 14 January 1797.
17 W.James: *The Naval History of Great Britain,* 1837 II, p.14.
18 M.Lewis: *A Social history of the Navy,* p.420.
19 *PRO ADM51 1210.*
20 *PRO ADM36 13145* Muster Records.
21 J.Skinner: *A West Country Tour,* p.78.
22 *PRO ADM36 13146.*

Chapter 3
1 *RCG* 28 August 1813.
2 *RCG* 7 August 1802.
3 W.Tuck: *Reminiscences of Cornwall,* p.19.
4 *RCG* 8 February 1806: 15 November 1806.
5 Quoted in AKH Jenkin: *Cornwall and its people* (London, 1932), p.151.
6 *RCG* 23 January 1805.
7 *RCG* 16 January 1802.
8 *RCG* 31 July, 7 August, 14 August 1802.
9 *RCG* 27 October 1806.
10 *WB* 12 February 1819.
11 *RCG* 23 October 1824.
12 *WB* 7 January 1825.
13 *RCG* 6 August 1825.
14 *RCG* 19 April 1828.

Chapter 4
1 *RCG* 12 April 1806.
2 A.Rowe: 'Cornish Men and Matters'; *WB* 16 August 1954.
3 *WB* 29 March 1819.
4 *WB* 3 January 1817.
5 *RCG* 30 August 1806.
6 *RCG* 30 August 1806.
7 *RCG* 9 August 1806.

8 *RCG* 9 August 1806.
9 D.Arundell: *The Critic at the Opera, passim.*
10 *RCG* 13 September 1806.
11 *RCG* 30 May 1807.
12 Quoted in R.Fiske: *English Theatre Music in the Eighteenth Century* (London 1973), p.629.
13 *ibid*:p.629.
14 *ibid*: p.271.
15 *RCG* 23 December 1808.
16 *RCG* 16 October 1808.
17 *RCG* 11 July 1807.
18 *RCG* 25 July 1807.
19 *RCG* 26 August 1809.
20 *RCG* 13 September 1806.
21 D.Arundell: *The Critic at the Opera*, p.303ff.
22 *WB* 20 August 1813: *RCG* 14 August 1813.
23 Reports from *WB* 3 September: *RCG* 28 August and 4 September 1813.

Chapter 5
1 Rev R.Polwhele: *Traditions and Recollections*,1826 I, p.96.
2 J.Forbes: 'Tour into Cornwall', *JRIC* IX, p.169.
3 Quoted by A.Rowe: *WB* 28 March 1957.
4 R.Polwhele: *Traditions and Recollections*, p.580.
5 *RCG* 25 July 1807.
6 Truro Buildings Research Group: *Pydar Street and the High Cross Area*, p.35.
7 *RCG* 18 October 1810.
8 *RCG* 10 November 1804.
9 *RCG* 5 September 1807.
10 *RCG* 16 April 1808.
11 *RCG* 8 February 1806.
12 *RCG* 1 September 1810.
13 *RCG* 15 September 1810.
14 *WB* 12 October 1810.
15 *RCG* 29 May 1806.
16 M.Kelly: *Reminiscences* [1826] (ed. R. Fiske, London 1975), p.235.
17 *WB* 7 August 1818.
18 *RCG* 10 March 1804: other reports, 24 December 1803, 28 January, 18 February & 7 April 1804.
19 *RCG* 19 April 1806.
20 *RCG* 1 June 1808.
21 *RCG* 9 June 1810.
22 *WB* 3 November 1815.
23 Truro Buildings Research Group: *Lemon Street and its Neighbourhood, passim.*
24 *WB* 19 December 1817.
25 *WB* 10 December 1819.

26 *WB* 1 December 1820.
27 *WB* 14 December 1821.
28 *WB* 7 November 1823.
29 *RCG* 11 May 1804.
30 *RCG* 28 October 1809.
31 *WB* 6 January 1815.
32 *RCG* 16 August 1818.
33 *WB* 12 November 1824.
34 *RCG* 5 April 1828.
35 *WB* 19 April 1816.
36 *WB* 11 April 1818.
37 *WB* 10 January 1817.
38 *WB* 27 March 1818.
39 *WB* 23 April 1823.

Chapter 6
 1 W.Tuck: *Reminiscences of Cornwall* p.18.
 2 *WB* 1 January 1819.
 3 *WB* 21 December 1821.
 4 *WB* 27 December 1822.
 5 *WB* 23 May 1823.
 6 *WB* 21 April 1826.
 7 *WB* 5 October 1810.
 8 *WB* 4 October 1811.
 9 *WB* 2 December 1821.
10 *RCG* 23 October 1824.
11 *WB* 3 December 1824.
12 *RCG* 1 January 1825.
13 *RCG* 27 October 1827.
14 *RCG* 31 July 1824.
15 *RCG* 10 June 1809.
16 *WB* 3 January 1817.
17 *WB* 10 January 1817.
18 *WB* 10 January 1817.

Chapter 7
 1 N.Temperley: *The Music of the English Parish Church* (Cambridge,1979), p.xvii.
 2 *ibid*: p.233.
 3 Donaldson: *The Bishopric of Truro: the first twenty five years, 1877-1902* (London 1902); quoted by Temperley: *op. cit.* p.196.
 4 A.L.Rowse: *A Cornish Childhood* (London 1942), p.32.
 5 N.Temperley: *op. cit.* p.3.
 6 A.L.Rowse: *op. cit.* p.24.
 7 Obituary in *The Gentleman's Magazine*: Vol.XIII New Series, MDCCCXL, 208-211.
 8 *ibid*.

9 Quoted by A.K.Jenkin: *Cornwall and its People* (London, 1932), pp.180-181.
10 *ibid.*, p.164.
11 N.Temperley: *op cit* p.4.
12 *ibid.*, p.253.
13 *RCG* 18 October 1823.
14 *WB* 27 July 1821.
15 W.Tuck: *Reminiscences of Cornwall*; p.4.

Chapter 8
1 ed. R.Jones: *West Country Tour*; pp. 87—90.
2 Canon J.Hammond: *A Cornish Parish*; p.144.
3 *WB* 12 November 1824.
4 *WB* 2 June 1826.
5 *WB* 21 July 1826.
6 For a full account of the contents of this collection see: R.J.McGrady: 'Bennett Swaffield's *Sacred Harmony*'; JRIC X, p.44-57.
7 *WB* 15 November 1822.

Chapter 9
1 S.Gilbert: *An Historical Survey of the County of Cornwall*; Vol II, p.716.
2 *WB* 5 September 1823: *RCG* 6 September 1823.
3 *WB* 4 October 1816.
4 J.Maclean: *Parochial and Family History of the Parish and Borough of Bodmin*, (London, 1870), p.53.
5 *WB* 21 December 1821.
6 *WB* 9 November 1821.
7 *WB* 21 December 1821.
8 *WB* 22 December 1822: 31 December 1824.
9 *WB* 31 May 1816.
10 *WB* 2 December 1821: 31 December 1824, *et cet.*
11 *WB* 11 November 1825.
12 J.L.Kempthorne: *Falmouth Parish Church* (Falmouth 1925), p.49-50.
13 W.L.Sumner: *The Organ* (London, 1975), p.187.
14 Full specifications from the Taunton MS and Spry lecture are given in Appendix A.
15 R.Polwhele: *Reminiscences in Prose and Verse* (1836) pp.36-37.
16 Glasgow University Library: Euing Music Collection, R.d.86 (99).
17 Most of the letter was originally written in the first person, but Hempel altered the text to convert it to the third person which he clearly felt was more appropriate to a dictionary entry. The original version, and occasional excised passages, are included in square brackets.
18 Vol.1, p.228.
19 Pigot: *National Commercial Directory*.

20 *WB* 22 July 1825.
21 F.W.B.Bullock: *A History of the Parish of St Mary, Truro, Cornwall* (Truro 1948) pp.109-111 *passim*.

Chapter 10

 1 C.S.Gilbert: *Historical Survey of the County of Cornwall*, II,p.816.
 2 Truro Buildings Research Group: *Pydar Street and the High Cross Area*; p.36.
 3 *RCG* 26 December 1801.
 4 *RCG* 17 April 1802.
 5 *RCG* 29 December 1809.
 6 *RCG* 30 May 1807.
 7 *RCG* 25 July 1807.
 8 *RCG* 17 February 1809.
 9 *RCG* 10 November 1810.
10 *WB* 9 November 1810.
11 *WB* 16 November 1810.
12 *WB* 21 December 1810.
13 *WB* 7 December 1810.
14 *WB* 3 May 1811.
15 *WB* 25 November 1825.
16 *WB* 26 January 1821.
17 *WB* 23 February 1821.
18 *WB* 19 June 1824.
19 *WB* 13 August 1824.
20 *WB* 14 January 1825.
21 *WB* 11 November 1825.
22 *RCG* 20 October 1825.
23 *WB* 16 December 1825.
24 *RCG* 20 October 1827.
25 *WB* 5 October 1827.
26 *WB* 5 October 1827.
27 *WB* 26 October 1827.
28 *WB* 9 November 1827.
29 *RCG* 24 November 1827.
30 *WB* 18 January 1828.
31 *RCG* 15 December 1827.
32 *RCG* 1 December 1827.
33 *RCG* 17 November 1827.
34 *WB* 12 October 1827.
35 *WB* 19 October 1827.
36 *WB* 9 November 1827.
37 *RCG* 13 October 1827.
38 *WB* 18 January 1828.

SELECT BIBLIOGRAPHY

Arundell, Dennis, *The Critic at the Opera* (London, 1957).

Beckford, William, *Italy with sketches of Spain and Portugal* (London, 1834).

Bennett, Charles, *Twelve Songs and a Cantata* (London, no date).

Boase, C.G and Courtney, W.P, *Bibliotheca Cornubiensis* (London 1878).

Buckingham, James Silk, *Autobiography* (London, 1855).

Bullock, F.W.B, *A History of the Parish of St. Mary, Truro, Cornwall* (Truro, 1948).

Couch, Jonathan, 'The Private Memoirs of Jonathan Couch' (ed. A. Wheeler) *JIRC* IX (1983), p.92.

Fiske, Roger, *English Theatre Music in the Eighteenth Century* (London 1973).

Forbes, James, 'Tour into Cornwall', *JIRC* IX (1983), p.146.

Francis, D., *Portugal 1715–1808* (London 1985).

Gentleman's Magazine, Obituary of Davies Gilbert; Vol.XIII New Series 1840, p.208.

Gilbert, C.S, *An Historical Survey of the County of Cornwall* (1817/1820).

Gilbert, Davies, *Some Ancient Christmas Carols with the Tunes to which they were formerly Sung in the West of England* (London, 2nd ed. 1823).

Hammond, Canon J, *A Cornish Parish being an Account of St. Austell* (London 1878).

Heard, *Gazetteer* (1817).

Hempel, C.W, *A Morning and an Evening Service* (London, no date).

—*Church Services and Anthems* (London, no date).

—*Sacred Melodies Adapted to the Psalms of David* (2 Editions, London, no date).

James, W, *The Naval History of Great Britain from the Declaration of War by France in 1793 . . .* (6 Vols., London 1837).

Jenkin, A.K.H, *Cornwall and its people* (London 1932; repr. 1945).

Kempthorne, J.L, *Falmouth Parish Church* (Falmouth 1925).

Kendall, Edward, *Six Voluntaries for the Harpsicord or Organ* (London 1775).

Lewis, Michael, *A Social history of the Navy 1793-1815* (London 1960).

Maclean, J, *Parochial and Family History of the Parish and Borough of Bodmin* (London 1870).

McGrady, Richard, 'Cornwall's Earliest Music Festivals 1806–1813'; *Cornish Studies* 3 (1975) p. 48.

—'Bennett Swaffield's *Sacred Harmony*'; *JIRC* X (1986–7), p. 44.

—'Joseph Emidy: An African in Cornwall'; *The Musical Times* (November, 1986) p. 619.

Mannix, D.P, *Black Cargoes* (London, 1963).

Parkinson, C Northcote, *Edward Pellew* (London, 1935).

Polwhele, Rev. R, *Traditions and Recollections* (1826).

—*Reminiscences in Prose and Verse* (1836).

Public Record Office Documents Relating to *The Indefatigable*:

ADM51 1109 Pellew's Log Feb 1795–Feb 1796.

ADM51 1171 Pellew's LogMar 1796–Feb 1797.

ADM51 1210 Pellew's Log Mar 1797–Feb 1798.

ADM51 1246 Pellew's Log Mar 1798–Feb 1799.

ADM51 1293 Curzon's Log Mar 1799–Feb 1800.

ADM36 13142 Muster Book 1795.

ADM36 13143 Muster Book 1796.

ADM36 13144 Muster Book 1796–1797.

ADM36 13145 Muster Book 1797–1798.

ADM36 13146 Muster Book 1798–1799.

Rodger, N.A.M, *The Wooden World: An Anatomy of the Georgian Navy* (London, 1986).

Rowe, Ashley, 'Cornish Men and Matters'; *WB* 16 August 1954, 28 March 1957.

Rowse, A.L. *A Cornish Childhood* (London, 1942).

Skinner, John, *A West Country Tour* (ed.R. Jones, Bradford on Avon, 1985).

Spry, E.J, 'Notes relating . . . to St. Mary's Church, Truro'; 22nd. Annual Report of the Royal Institution of Cornwall, 1840, p.841.

Sumner, J.L, *The Organ* (London, 1975).

Swaffield, Bennett, *Twenty Five Original Melodies, Adapted to Selected Parts of the New Version of Psalms . . .* (London, 1822).

Taunton, Dr Richard, Manuscript Notes on the History of Truro (Library of the Royal Institution of Cornwall).

Temperley, Nicholas, *The Music of the English Parish Church* (Cambridge, 1979).

Trade Directories, *Universal British Directory*: (1791).

[Pigot and Co.] *Commercial Directory for Cornwall*: 1823.

National Commercial Directory: 1830 & 1844.

Tuck, William R. *Reminiscences of Cornwall* (Truro, no date).

Truro Buildings Research Group, *Pydar Street and the High Cross Area* (Truro, no date).

—*Lemon Street and its Neighbourhood* (Truro, no date).

INDEX

Arthur Mr: leader of Cornwall band
  concert at Bodmin 80
  clarinet concerto at Lostwithiel 76, 82
Ashley, John and family: festivals 50, 56
assemblies 63-76
  Bodmin 43
  Truro 43, 63
  outdoor activities 68, 82
  Lostwithiel 82
  Penzance 66

Beckford, William
  Falmouth, visit to 7
  Portuguese social and musical life 16-20
Bennett, Charles: blind organist and
    composer 113-17
Bodmin
  assemblies 43
  concerts 80-1
  Lutman, organist 80, 111
  organ 110-11
  prison and prisoners 9
Brazilian *modinhas* 19
Buckingham, James Silk
  biography 9-11
  Emidy as music teacher 10, 42
  Emidy as violinist 40, 42
  musical accomplishments 10
  views on impressment and slavery 27,
    146
  visits Salomon 144-6
Byfield: organ builder 110, 113, 150-1

Callington: organ 109
Camborne
  church music 77, 101-2
  harmonic society 77
  organ 109
Catalani, Angelica: singer 58-60
carols 93-8
Christiana: 'professor' of pianoforte
  fees 39
  appearance in festival 59

choirs 50
  St Austell 105-8
church and chapel bands 91-2, 101
concerts
  Bodmin 80
  Falmouth 10, 42,
  Helston 80-1
  Lostwithiel 76, 81-3
  St Austell 106-7
  Truro 68-76
  Wadebridge 80
Cornwall
  Christmas festivities 92, 96
  Incledon's visit 55-6
  isolation, artistic 5
    travel 5
  music festivals 48-61
  tourism 6
Couch, Jonathan of Polperro 8
Crowan: organ and organist 109, 110

dancing
  balls 66, 68
  display at Penzance 66
  popular dances 67-8
Dawson, Mr: comedian and theatre
    manager 132-41
Dickons, Mrs: singer 51, 53, 57
Droits de l'homme, action with *Indefatigable*,
    30-3
Dutton, wreck of 30

Emidy, Joseph Antonia
  abilities as violinist 40
  advertisements as teacher 40-1
  Bodmin, concert performance 80
  Buckingham, meeting with 10
  Camborne harmonic society 77
  children 41
    Cecilia Hutchins, daughter of JA;
    Benjamin, fourth son of JA;
    James Hutchings, third son of JA;
    Joseph, eldest son of JA;

Richard, fifth son of JA;
Thomas Hutchins, second son of JA;
compositions 45, 71-2, 73, 144-6
compositions played by Salomon 145
concerts 42, 45-6, 71-3, 80-2
Falmouth, settles in 39
guitar and mandolin 40, 45
harmonic societies 41-2, 71-3
Helston concerts 80-1
Indefatigable, capture and duties aboard 25-36
Lisbon 17
marriage 41
obituaries 148
painting of 70-1
physical description 40, 41
slave 16
teaching music 40
theatre, possible involvement with 142
tombstone 1
Truro
  concerts in 71-3
  move to 72

Faning, Roger: organist at Helston 111
concerts 81
Falmouth
  coach services 5
  concerts 10, 42-7
  diversions 7
  Emidy 39, 41-2, 45
  Fisher, Samuel: actor-manager 129
  harmonic society 10, 41, 45-7
  Kendall, Edward: organist 112
  naval presence 8, 39, 46
  organ and organists 59, 109, 111, 112
  port 6
  prisoners 9, 34
  Sharp, Mr: organist and teacher 111
  theatre 45, 127, 128-9
festivals 48-61
Fisher, Samuel: actor-manager 129-32
French officers 9, 34

Giddy, Davies *see* Gilbert, Davies
Gilbert, Davies 95-8
Griglietti, Signora: singer 51-3

harmonic societies 40, 83
  Camborne 77
  Falmouth 10, 41-7

Helston 81
Truro 45, 68-76
Harrison: dancing master and organist, 113
Helston
  concerts 80-1
  Faning 81, 111
  'Forey Dance' 97
  organ and organists 109, 111
Hempel, Charles Frederick: vocalist, organist and composer, son of CW
  concerts 80, 81, 122
  move to Scotland 122
Hempel, Charles William: organist and composer, father of CF
  autobiographical letter 117-19
  appearances in festivals 57, 60
  compositions 60, 73, 118-21
  concerts in Truro 73-5
  full-time musician 118
  psalm settings 119-20
  services and anthems 120-1
  Truro organ, opinion of 112, 150-1
Hughes, Mr: theatre manager 131
Hutchins, Jennifer; wife of Joseph Emidy 41

Incledon, Charles: singer 53-6
Indefatigable 23-36
  action with *Droits de l'homme* 30-3
  refitting
    Portsmouth 24
    Lisbon 24-6
    Plymouth 30
  damaged off Cape Finisterre 24
  Pellew's command 23
  sails from Lisbon 29

Jacobwitch, Mr: vocalist 81

Kendall, Edward: organist 112
Kenwyn Parish Church
  Emidy's tombstone 1
  organ installed 100
Kollman, Augustus: musical theorist, uncle of CW Hempel 117

Launceston
  Methodist celebrations 101
  organ and organist 109, 110
  theatre 140
  Lisbon 17-20

Loder, John: music festivals 59-60
Lostwithiel
  concerts 76, 81-3
  regatta 82
Lutman, John: organist at Bodmin 79, 111
  concerts 80

militia bands 43-4, 46, 82, 129, 140
music teachers
  Christiana 39
  Emidy 40
  Falmouth, scarcity of, 40
  fees 39
  Sharp 111
  Sholl 110
  Swaffield 105
Murrish, William 98

organs 90, 109-23; *see also* organists
  barrel 91, 105
  Bodmin 109, 110-11
  Callington 109
  Camborne 101, 109
  Crowan 109
  Falmouth 109
  Helston 109
  Kenwyn 100
  Launceston 109
  Penzance 109, 110
  St Austell 106
  St Ives 109
  Truro 112-13, 150-1
  Veryan 109
organists *see also* organs
  advertisements for 110, 111
  Bennett 114-17
  Bodmin 80
  Falmouth 80
  Lutman 80
  Harrison 113
  Hempel 113, 117-22
  Putten, death of 110
  Sharp 80, 111
  Sholl, death of 110
  Swaffield 102-8
  Thomas, Mr (Crowan), suicide of 110
  Truro organists 113-23

parish churches, music of 89-102
  Kenwyn 1, 100
  Truro 112-23

St Austell 99, 104-8
St Day 99
St Germans 99
  Penzance 100
Pellew, Sir Edward
  action with *Droits de l'homme* 30-3
  command of *Indefatigable* 23-36
  command of *L'Impetueux* 35
  knighthood 23
  prisoners in his command 9, 34
Penryn
  Christiana, music teacher 39
  concert 45
Penzance
  church music 100
  concert 81
  dancing display 66
  mishaps in the theatre 67
  organ and organists 109, 110
philharmonic societies *see* harmonic societies
Polperro 8
Polwhele, Rev Richard
  account of Truro organist 114
  opinion of Truro social life 64
Portugal
  slave trade 15-16
  social and musical life 16-20
psalms
  domestic performance 98
  settings by Hempel 119-20
    by Swaffield 107-8
  singing 92-3, 98-9
  texts 92, 107
Putten, William: organist 110

Rauzzini, Venanzio: singer and teacher 54
Royal Navy
  allowances and pay 30, 36
  casualties and illness 33-4
  foreign nationals aboard British ships 28
  frigates 23
  impressment 27
  landsmen 29
  music and dancing 26

St Austell
  barrel organ installed 105
  chapel music 92-3
  parish church choir 102-8
  psalm singing 99
  Swaffield 102-8

St Day 99
St Germans 99
St Ives 109
Salomon, Johann Peter: violinist and
    impresario 144-6
Sandys, William: carol collector 97
Sharp, Mr: organist and teacher 80, 111
Sholl, William: organist and music teacher
    110
Slave trade
    Buckingham's views 27, 146
    Portuguese 15-16
Spry EJ: description of Byfield organ 150-1
Swaffield, Bennett 102-8

Tate and Brady psalm texts 92, 107
Taunton, Dr Richard 49, 82, 122, 150-1
    Truro organ and organists 112, 113,
        122-3, 150-1
theatre 127-42
    critic's views 136-41
    company members 136-9
    Dawson, Mr: comedian and theatre
        manager 132-42
    Falmouth 45, 127, 129, 132
    Fisher, Samuel: actor-manager 128-32
    Hughes, Mr: theatre manager 131
    Launceston 140
    music in 129, 130, 131, 134-6, 141
    novelties 131, 133
    orchestral standards 136, 140-1
    plays produced 129, 131, 134
    prices 131
    professional theatre, attitude to 127, 130
    tours 132
    Truro 128, 129-42
    Weber opera produced 134-6
Truro
    assemblies 43, 63-76

balls 66
Bennett 114-17
concerts 45, 63-76
Christiana, music teacher 39
Emidy 71-3
festivals 48-61
harmonic society 68-76
    painting of 70-1
Hempel, CW 73-5, 117-22
military and naval presence 43, 65
organ and organists 109, 112-23, 150-1
river trips 68
Sholl, music teacher 110
social character 63-4
theatre 128
    critical controversy 137-41
    Dawson's seasons 132-42
    building of 128
    Fisher's seasons 129-32
    refurbishment 132
    Weber opera produced 134-6
White, Mrs 75-6
Trist, Tryphena (Mrs Pendarves): music
    collection 84
Tuck, William
    church music in Camborne 77, 101-2
    Emidy in Camborne 77
    Emidy's capture 26, 77
    Emidy as violinist 40, 77
    harmonic society 79

Wadebridge 80
Warren, Sir John Borlase 23
Weber: *Der Freischütz*, performances 134-6
White, Mr: Cornwall Militia Band 73, 82
White, Mrs: singer
    concerts in Truro 75-6
    concert in Lostwithiel 76, 82-3